Battle Orders • 27

The Roman Army of the Punic Wars 264–146 BC

Nic Fields

Consultant Editor Dr Duncan Anderson • *Series editors* Marcus Cowper and Nikolai Bogdanovic

First published in Great Britain in 2007 by Osprey Publishing,
Midland House, West Way, Botley, Oxford OX2 0PH, UK
443 Park Avenue South, New York, NY 10016, USA
E-mail: info@ospreypublishing.com

A CIP catalogue record for this book is available from the British Library

ISBN 978 1 84603 145 8

Editorial by Ilios Publishing Ltd, Oxford, UK (www.iliospublishing.com)
Page layout by Boundford.com, Huntingdon. UK
Index by Alan Thatcher
Typeset in GillSans and Stone Serif
Originated by United Graphics, Singapore
Printed in China through Bookbuilders

07 08 09 10 11   10 9 8 7 6 5 4 3 2 1

FOR A CATALOGUE OF ALL BOOKS PUBLISHED BY OSPREY MILITARY AND
AVIATION PLEASE CONTACT:

NORTH AMERICA
Osprey Direct, c/o Random House Distribution Center, 400 Hahn Road,
Westminster, MD 21157
E-mail: info@ospreydirect.com

ALL OTHER REGIONS
Osprey Direct UK, P.O. Box 140 Wellingborough, Northants, NN8 2FA, UK
E-mail: info@ospreydirect.co.uk

Key to military symbols

Double consular army	Consular army	Praetorian army	Legio/ala
xxxx	xxx	xx	x

Cohors	Manipulus	Centuria/turma	Turma subunit
III	II	I	●●●

Infantry	Cavalry	Unit with part detached (-)	Reinforced unit (+)

Key to unit identification

Unit identifier — Parent unit — Commander

Key to first names (*praenomeninis*)

A.	Aulus
Ap.	Appius
C.	Caius
Cn.	Cnaeus
D.	Decimus
L.	Lucius
M.	Marcus
M'.	Manius
P.	Publius
Q.	Quintus
Ser.	Servius
Sex.	Sextus
Sp.	Spurius
T.	Titus
Ti.	Tiberius

Contents

Introduction   4
Conquest of Italy • First Punic War

Roman military organization   16
The Livian legion • The Polybian legion • Maniple • Light infantry • Cavalry • Citizen-militia

Socii military organization   28
Ala • *Cohors* • Cavalry

Command and control   31
Legion command • Centuriate • Junior officers • Command and control in action

Roman Army in battle   41
Roman tactical doctrine and practice • Legion • *Socii* • Light troops • Cavalry

Engineering   52
Marching camps • Roads • Siegecraft

Second Punic War   57
Hannibal's revenge • Hannibal's aims • The long struggle • The Trebbia, genius at work • Lake Trasimene, the perfect ambush
Cannae, a lesson in annihilation • The Metaurus, the beginning of the end • Ilipa, Iberia lost • Zama, a lesson learnt

Military superpower   86

Chronology   88

Ancient authors   91
Appian (b. AD 95) • Cassius Dio (b. AD 164) • Diodorus Siculus (b. *c.*80 BC)

Bibliography   93

Glossary   94

Index   95

Introduction

Before the Second Punic War (218–201 BC) Rome's influence extended no further northwards than the Alps and no further southwards than Sicily. Within a century, however, the seeds of empire had been sown in Iberia, Africa and the Hellenistic east. As an instrument of conquest the Roman middle-republican army was the most successful of its day, and established standards of discipline, organization and efficiency that set a benchmark for the later armies of imperial Rome.

The wars fought by early Rome had consisted of small-scale raids and cattle rustling, with perhaps the occasional battle between armies. The latter were little more than warrior bands formed by an aristocrat, his kin and clients, such as the clan-army of the Fabii with its 306 *cognati et sodales* – 'clansmen and companions' (Livy 2.49.4, cf. Dionysios 9.15.3). The clan leader fought for

personal glory, his followers out of loyalty to him and, of course, the prospect of portable booty. Destitute as they are of historical credibility, many of the heroic tales of Rome's early history recorded by Livy (books 1–3) may have their origins in the ballads composed to celebrate the warlike deeds of these clans (*gentes*) during this period of border forays.

The predatory behaviour of the early Romans is ideally illustrated by the raids and counter-raids conducted against the petty hill-tribes of the Volsci, Aequi, Sabini and Hernici, what Livy labels the frequent instances of *nec certa pax nec bellum fuit* – 'neither assured peace nor open war' (2.21.1). However, a major development came with the adoption by Rome of the Greek-style phalanx, composed of citizens wealthy enough to equip themselves with the full panoply of a hoplite, probably some time in the 6th century BC. Though Diodoros says (23.2.1) the phalanx came by way of the Etruscans, in all probability this change owes its origins to the Greek colonies that fringed the coasts of southern Italy.

Livy (1.42–43) and Dionysios of Halikarnassos (4.13–23), both writing in the late 1st century BC, attribute a major reform of Rome's socio-political and military organization to the popular king, Servius Tullius (traditionally 579–534 BC). His first consideration was the creation of a citizen army, and the most important point was to induce the citizens to adequately arm themselves. So a census of all adult male citizens recorded the value of their property and divided them accordingly into classes (*classes*). Whether or not Servius actually existed, the archaeological record does suggest that the Romans adopted hoplite equipment around this time, so the annalistic tradition may be broadly accurate.

These bone plaques from Palestrina, 4th century BC, give a good impression of early Roman equipment. Much of it is Hellenistic, and each warrior appears to have a large, round shield resting against their legs. These men would not have been out of place in a hoplite phalanx. (Author's collection)

In Livy (1.42.5–14) the Servian classes I, II and III essentially fought with hoplite panoply. The notable exception being that members of class I armed themselves with the round *clipeus*, that is, the *aspis* carried by Greek hoplites, a soup-bowl shaped shield, approximately 90cm in diameter and clamped to the left arm. Classes II and III, on the other hand, used the oval *scutum*, an Italic shield that was very much like the *thureos* common to peltasts of later Hellenistic armies. Classes IV and V were armed as skirmishers, the last class perhaps carrying nothing more than a sling.

This system provided the basis of the *comitia centuriata*, the 'assembly in centuries' at which the citizens voted to declare war or accept a peace treaty, elected the consuls, praetors and censors, the senior magistrates of Rome, and tried capital cases. Gathering on the *campus Martius* (Field of Mars), an open area outside the original boundary (*pomoerium*) of the city, its structure exemplified the ideal of a citizen militia in battle array, men voting and fighting together in the same units. This assembly operated on a 'timocratic principle', and Gibbon describes it well:

In the purer ages of the commonwealth, the use of arms was reserved for those ranks of citizens who had a country to love, a property to defend, and some share in enacting those laws, which it was their interest, as well as a duty, to maintain.
Decline and Fall I.36

Italic bronze plaque, 5th century BC, depicting a warrior holding a large, round shield (Greek *aspis*, Latin *clipeus*). The rest of his hoplite panoply consists of a crested pot helmet, greaves and two spears, one apparently with a larger head than the other. (Author's collection)

The timocratic principle meant that only those who could afford arms could vote, which meant the *comitia centuriata* was in effect an assembly of property-owners-cum-citizen-soldiers. Yet the Servian Army of Livy and Dionysios of Halikarnassos does not appear in their battle accounts.

Citizen-hoplites are, by and large, peasant-farmers and could afford to spend only a few summer weeks on campaign before they needed to return to their fields. As a result conflicts were of short duration, usually decided by a single clash between opposing forces. The principle of a citizen-militia was retained at Rome, long after states in the Hellenistic world had come to rely on soldiers who were mainly professionals, highly trained and disciplined. However, the Romans modified the system to cope with demands of wars that were being fought farther and farther from home, and the intimate link between hoplite warfare and agricultural year was broken. From the beginning of the 4th century BC Rome paid its citizen-soldiers for the duration of a campaign (Livy 4.59.11, Diodoros 14.16.5). The wage was not high, and certainly did not make soldiering a career, but it supported the citizen during his military service by covering his basic living expenses. Men now served in the army until they were discharged, usually at the end of a campaign, which might last more than one season.

Conquest of Italy

During the 5th and first part of the 4th centuries BC the Romans were preoccupied with the circle of peoples in the immediate neighbourhood of Rome: the Etrusci (Etruscans) to the north, the Latini (Latins[1]) to the south, and the Volsci and Aequi to the east. Yet the initial steps of conquest was arrested by the land-hungry Gauls who, having spilled over the Alps and settled in the fertile Po Valley, launched raids deep into the Italian Peninsula. On the banks of the Allia, a tributary of the Tiber just 18km north of Rome, the Senonian Gauls utterly trounced the army sent to repel them (Livy 5.38) and the city itself was sacked (390 BC). Fortunately for the Romans, however, the Gauls were primarily out for plunder not for land, and promptly withdrew northwards with their spoils.

By the middle of the 4th century BC the Romans had subdued the Latins, who had settled in the open country south of the lower reaches of the Tiber and gave it its name of Latium, and the Sabini, who lived in the mountains bordering on Latium. They now controlled the northern end of the main route that led southwards to the ager Falernus, the lush plain of Campania. The Campani, who occupied this fertile region, were descendants of the Oscan-speaking Lucani who had come down from the Apennines to fill the vacuum left by the withdrawal of the Etruscans. The Oscan military ethic encouraged wars of conquest, but in these rich lands the Lucani had established something

---

1 This is the ethno-cultural group to which the Romans mainly belong. In the Early Iron Age these people had consisted of a group of communities (traditionally 30) who spoke Latin, and who were united by common cults, especially of Iuppiter Latiaris. Archaeology has shown that they also had some distinctive artefacts and burial practices. By the 6th century BC the Latin communities were grouped into a political and military league.

like an ascendancy that abjured the memory of their warrior-fathers. Thus the warlike Samnites, the Oscans who inhabited the mountainous region of the Abruzzi (Samnium), in turn started harassing their former conquerors who now formed the aristocracy of Campania, especially in its great and prosperous city of Capua. Eventually, this allowed the Romans to exploit the worsening situation and support the Campani against the Samnites, an action that provoked the First Samnite War (343–341 BC). Hard on the heels of this conflict followed the Latin War (341–338 BC), which saw the perverted spectacle of Romans fighting against their allies of yesterday who wished, quite naturally, to share equally in the spoils of war. After these two conflicts Roman control over Latium and Campania was finally asserted.

Regrettably this is really all we know of Rome's initial dealings with the Samnites and the first war, and even this is veiled in legend. The historical record, however, is less ambiguous for the Second Samnite War (327–304 BC), described by Livy (books 7–10) in his inescapable but entertaining dramatic style. When the Italiote-Greek citizens of Neapolis (Naples) appealed to Rome against the Samnites, who had occupied their *polis* with a garrison, the second war was set in train. This conflict was particularly hard fought, and the Roman Army was to suffer a serious and humiliating reverse at the Caudine Forks (321 BC). The unfavourable treaty that followed this defeat, a disaster to rank alongside the Allia rout, was soon broken when Rome resumed the struggle (316 BC). Despite a number of setbacks, Rome at length emerged triumphant. It now controlled nearly all Samnium and had planted a handful of colonies in southern Campania and western Apulia. The abandonment of the Greek phalanx organization and the introduction of the manipular system may have been learned through experience, fighting in the rough, mountainous terrain of the Apennines during this war.

This Tarentine stater, c.381–345 BC (Vlasto 381), shows a Greek horseman bearing a small shield with a flat rim and convex centre. It is possible that this type of shield, flimsily constructed out of ox-hide, was also used by the cavalry of early Rome. (Author's collection)

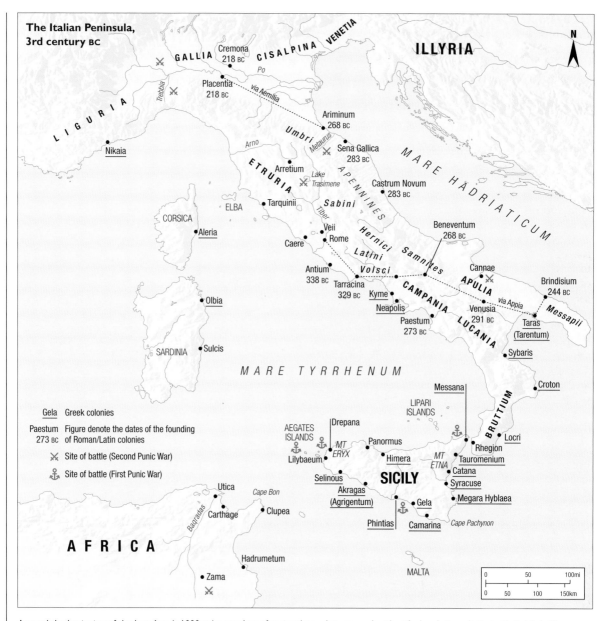

The Italian Peninsula, 3rd century BC

Gela — Greek colonies

Paestum 273 BC — Figure denote the dates of the founding of Roman/Latin colonies

✕ — Site of battle (Second Punic War)

⚓ — Site of battle (First Punic War)

Around the beginning of the Iron Age (c.1000 BC) a number of regional populations can be identified and given distinct ethnic labels. They can be differentiated partly by their language, and partly by distinctive customs, including such things as the use of characteristic artefacts, burial practices and religious cults: the Etruscans, originally settled in a large area north of Rome between the Anio and Tiber rivers, and organized into a loose confederation of largely autonomous cities; the Latins, the ethno-cultural group to which the Romans mainly belong; the Oscans (Samnites, Lucani, Bruttii), settled in the Apennine mountains, who spoke a language that was closely related to Latin, but had some distinctive characteristics; and the Greeks, who, beginning in the 8th century BC, had established colonies on the fertile coastal plains of Sicily and southern Italy. So Italy in the Late Iron Age was a melting pot of different ethnic and tribal groupings. In the late 5th century BC, the brew was violently stirred up by the arrival of Celts from central Europe where the Celtic La Tène culture had developed around 500 BC.

Rome had gradually grown in size from its earliest history, absorbing other peoples into the population, but it was only in the second half of the 4th century BC that its expansion began in earnest. Then, in less than a century, the Romans defeated the Etruscans, Samnites, the Gallic tribes south of the Po and, finally, the various peoples of southern Italy. Defeats were suffered in all of these conflicts, but Rome persevered and continued the struggle until victory was achieved. Some land was expropriated from the defeated peoples and used to establish colonies of Roman (*coloniae civium Romanorum*) and Latin citizens (*coloniae Latinae*), which acted as garrisons in each area. In this case the state would divide the land (*ager publicus*) into small plots for *viritim* distribution to individual peasant-farmers. The actual 'bricks and mortar' of a garrison colony was similar in layout to a military camp, and most often built upon a 'virgin' or 'green-field' site. In time many, such as Ostia and Puteoli, were to expand far outside the original fortified nucleus or *castrum*. However, in most cases the conquered communities were absorbed into Rome's network of allies, and in their turn provided soldiers to fight in Rome's wars. By the beginning of the 3rd century BC Rome was without doubt the strongest power in the Italian Peninsula.

The Third Samnite War (298–290 BC) signalled the demise of the Samnites as a free people. The Romans crushed a coalition of Etruscans, Umbri, Samnites and Senonian Gauls at Sentinum in Umbria (295 BC), and finally, five years on, the Romans successfully subdued the whole of Samnium and impinged upon Lucania. It was now felt from one end of the Apennines to the other that Rome was the chief power in Italy and, by the turn of the 2nd century BC, it was obvious to contemporary Graeco-Roman writers that the peninsula's real frontier was created by the Alps. The references made by Polybios (6.17.2) and Cato the Censor (*De Agricultura* fr. 85 P) leave no doubt about this point.

Thus by becoming 'romanized', the peninsula was unified. Yet this unification of Italy was not only a matter of adopting Roman political and cultural attitudes, but also one of integration according to the concept the various Italic peoples had of the geographical area that was known as *Italia*. Thus romanization may have had the merit of being ambiguous, like many things Roman, but it surely did not stand for 'togas and Latin'.

The final phase of the conquest culminated in the sack of the Italiote-Greek *polis* of Taras (272 BC), a punishment meted out by the Romans for having invited to Italy Pyrrhos of Epeiros (281 BC), a kinsman by marriage of the royal house of Alexander the Great and an outstanding soldier of fortune. Polybios puts this action of the Tarentines down to 'the arrogance that is so often induced by prosperity' (8.24.1), yet it was nothing new for, around 350 BC, democratic Taras had adopted the policy of employing mercenary captains to fight its foreign wars. By doing so Taras was hoping to contain and control the mounting pressure from a wide coalition of Italic tribes, including the Lucani, Bruttii and Messapii. Apart from the larger-than-life Pyrrhos, the role call of illustrious *condottieri* included Archidamos (343 BC), Akrotatos (315 BC) and Kleonymos (303 BC), all Spartans of royal blood, as well as Alexander the Molossian (334 BC), the protégé of Philip II of Macedon and Pyrrhos' predecessor as king of Epeiros, and Agathokles (320 BC), the future tyrant of Syracuse.

The Etruscans, the most cultured of the Italic races, extended their influence northwards nearly to the Alps, and southwards over Campania. From Etruria Rome borrowed many ideas and concepts, including those for military and political purposes. The detail on this 3rd-century alabaster cinerary urn (Palermo, Museo Archeologico, 8461) depicts two Etruscan warriors. (Author's collection)

Fourth-century bronze statuette (Paris, musée du Louvre, Br 124) of a Samnite warrior, believed to have been found on Sicily. He wears an Attic-type helmet with holes that once held feathers, characteristic Oscan triple-disc cuirass, broad Oscan belt and greaves. His shield and spear are missing. (Esther Carré)

Because it had been the dominant power of southern Italy, Rome made absolutely sure that Taras would remain humbled. Its territory was confiscated and made public land (*ager publicus*), and the maritime trade that had made it prosperous passed across the promontory to Brundisium (Brindisi), which was soon made a Latin colony (244 BC) and there it has remained ever since. With the defeat of Taras (Tarentum to the Romans, now Taranto), according to Florus, 'all Italy enjoyed peace' (*Epitome* 1.14.1). Peace, however, would be short lived, as the Romans were about to cross to Sicily, which was the first country beyond the shores of Italy on which they set foot, and cross swords with a potential rival in the western Mediterranean, the old Phoenician colony of Carthage.[2]

---

2 Kart-Hadasht, or New City, as the Carthaginians called it, Karchedon to the Greeks, and thus Carthago to the Romans, Carthage had been founded, according to Timaios of Tauromenium (*FGrHist* 566 F 60), in 814 BC either direct from Tyre or as a sub-colony of the earlier Utica.

First Punic War

The fire that had been slowly smouldering for some time was kindled into flame in an unexpected manner. After the death of Agathokles of Syracuse (289 BC), a band of his Campanian mercenaries found themselves without employment. Instead of returning home, they decided to seize the *polis* of Messana (Messina), facing across the narrow straits to the toe of Italy, from its Greek inhabitants and to live as an independent community of brigands (Polybios 1.7.1–5). Their position was further strengthened by a similar seizure of Rhegion (Reggio di Calabria), across the straits in Italy, by a force of Roman troops made up of Campanian 'citizens without the vote' (Polybios 1.7.6). Calling themselves the Mamertini or 'sons of Mamers', the Oscan version of the war-god Mars, they harried north-eastern Sicily until finally defeated by Hieron II, the new tyrant of Syracuse (Polybios 1.9.7–9, cf. Diodoros 22.13.6). Thereupon some of them turned to the Carthaginians and offered to put themselves and Messana in their hands (265 BC). At the same time, however, another faction among the Mamertini had sent envoys to Rome seeking protection as Campani and so as a kindred people, and they likewise proposed to surrender Messana. The acceptance of this appeal by the Senate was the spark that fired the train. The immediate cause of the First Punic War is thus clear.

The fundamental causes of the First Punic War, however, are not so clear, but for once we have, in Polybios' account (1.10.1–11.2), some of the opinions that were supposed to have been aired in the Senate at the time. It seems in Polybios' view the overriding consideration in the minds of those senators who advocated acceptance of the appeal, was fear less the island pass finally under Punic control and 'allow the Carthaginians as it were to build a bridge for crossing to Italy' (1.10.9). We have no means of knowing whether the Carthaginians had any intentions of interfering in Italy. Nevertheless, Rome must have been sensitive about the attitude of Italiote-Greek *poleis* of the south

Italic Negau helmet (Arezzo, Museo Archeologico Nazionale), 5th century BC. This was the commonest form of helmet in Etruria at this time, and the use of Italic armour hardly affected the function of the Greek-style phalanx as long as the front-rank warriors bore the *clipeus*. (Esther Carré)

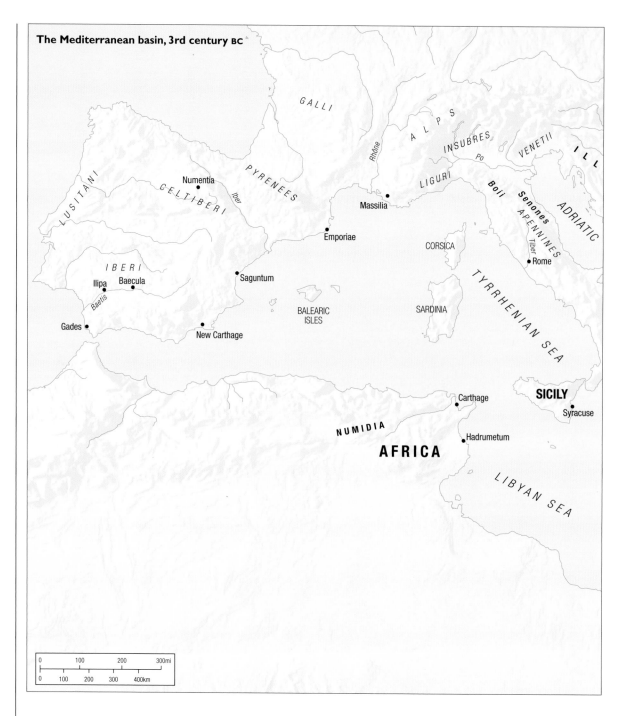

The Mediterranean basin, 3rd century BC

GALLI

ALPS

INSUBRES

Rhône

VENETII

LIGURI

ILL

Boii

Senones

APENNINES

ADRIATIC

PYRENEES

Numentia

Massilia

CELTIBERI

Iber

Emporiae

CORSICA

Rome

Tiber

LUSITANI

TYRRHENIAN SEA

IBERI

Saguntum

Ilipa   Baecula

BALEARIC
ISLES

SARDINIA

Baetis

Gades

New Carthage

SICILY

Carthage

Syracuse

NUMIDIA

Hadrumetum

AFRICA

LIBYAN SEA

| 0 | 100 | 200 | 300mi |
| 0 | 100 | 200 | 300 | 400km |

Since Alexander the Great had failed to provide an adult male heir to succeed him, his premature demise was to turn the Hellenic world upside down. The 47 years from 323 BC onwards witnessed the dismemberment of Alexander's empire by his generals, who, taking full advantage of this dynastic problem, reasserted the inherent disloyalty of the Macedonian nobility. This chaotic period was dominated by the *Diadochi* (Successors), an extremely complex era involving a kaleidoscope of larger-than-life personalities and shifting alliances. However, by the year 276 BC there was three major Hellenistic dynasties with which Rome was eventually to do business, the Ptolemies in Egypt, the Seleukids in Syria, and the Antigonids in Macedonia and Greece.

Also part of the Hellenic world, but politically divided, were the Greek communities of Sicily and southern Italy (Magna Graeca) as well those dotted around the coasts of southern Gaul and Iberia. The Iberi (Iberians) in the south, Celtiberi in the north, and the Lusitani in the west occupied the last. All three peoples were tribal but, much like the Liguri of north-western Italy, these tribes were much more fragmented socially than their Gallic counterparts who, known to the Greeks as *Keltai* and the Romans as *Galli*, populated Gaul and northern Italy (Gallia Cisalpina).

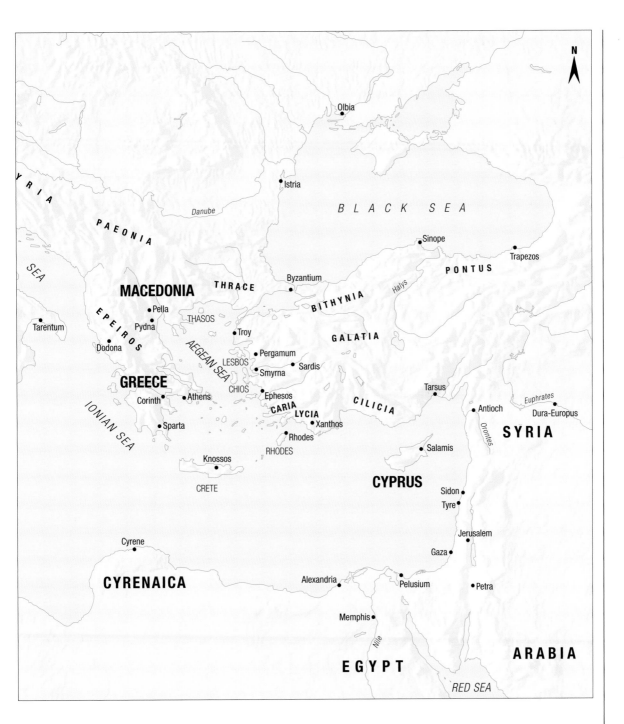

At the beginning of the century Carthage was undisputedly the greatest power in the western Mediterranean, the Romans only coming to prominence, at least in the eyes of the literate Greek world, following their stubborn resistance to and eventual victory over Pyrrhos of Epeiros (280–275 BC). Yet they remained entirely an Italian power. The Carthaginians, on the other hand, enjoyed the fruits of their hegemony over the whole coast of northern Africa from Cyrenaica to the Atlantic, southern and eastern Iberia, the Balearic Islands and the islands of Corsica, Sardinia and Sicily. They thus maintained a powerful navy, a highly skilled and professional force, both to deal with pirates and to discourage others from competing with their traders. Closer to home the Carthaginians controlled the whole of the Hermaia Peninsula (Cape Bon), and much of the fertile land watered by the Baqradas (Oued Medjerda) and beyond to the south-west, more or less as far as the present frontier between Tunisia and Algeria. Thus Carthage remained the richest city in the Mediterranean world, according to Polybios (18.35.9), even after it had twice been defeated by Rome.

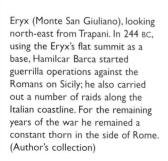

Etruscan cinerary urn in tufa (Florence, Museo Archeologico, 5744) from Volterra, 2nd century BC. The relief depicts two warriors, one bearing the Graeco-Etruscan *clipeus* (right) and the other the Italic *scutum* (left). Both these shield types were used in the Greek-style phalanx of early Rome. (Author's collection)

with which it had so recently been at war, and there is the later annalistic tradition that a Punic fleet had gone to the aid of Taras, which was still held by Pyrrhos' lieutenant Milo, during the latter stages of the Roman siege (Livy *Peiochae* 14, Dio fr. 43, Zonaras 8.6, Orosius 4.3.1–2, Ampelius 46.2, cf. Livy 21.10.8).

Thus Roman fears, though perhaps groundless, may have been quite genuine. It should also be noted that the acceptance of the Mamertini appeal did not mark any new departure in Roman foreign policy: it had long been characteristic of the Senate to accept such appeals, naturally, when it suited. The Carthaginians, for their part, could have avoided war had they been prepared to accept a *fait accompli* in Messana, but they must

Eryx (Monte San Giuliano), looking north-east from Trapani. In 244 BC, using the Eryx's flat summit as a base, Hamilcar Barca started guerrilla operations against the Romans on Sicily; he also carried out a number of raids along the Italian coastline. For the remaining years of the war he remained a constant thorn in the side of Rome. (Author's collection)

have calculated that if the Romans were allowed to interfere there, this might lead to further encroachment elsewhere in Sicily. At the same time, they had every reason to expect success: their navy could dominate the waters around Sicily and control of the island was ultimately bound to depend on seapower. It appears that the prime reason for the war was the mutual fear in both Rome and Carthage of the other's growing power, each believing their only long-term security lay in weakening the other's power (Dio 11.1–4, Zonaras 8.8).

Polybios describes the First Punic War as 'the longest, most continuous and the greatest war of which we have knowledge' (1.63.4), and the first round in the struggle between Rome and Carthage would rage for some 23 years, mainly fought out in and around the coasts of Sicily. It was chiefly remarkable for the Roman achievement in not only building up a navy, but in winning all the major naval engagements (Mylae 260 BC, Ecnomus 256 BC) save one (Drepana 249 BC), culminating in the decisive victory off the Aegates Islands (March 241 BC). The struggle at sea was the greatest naval war in antiquity, with fleets of more than 300 oared warships crewed by over 100,000 sailors, and at the end of it Rome, a nation of alleged landlubbers, replaced Carthage as the most powerful maritime state in the western Mediterranean. This is a fact that is often forgotten, but does go partway to explain Rome's eventual domination over all the lands of the Mediterranean basin (Polybios 1.20.6–14).

Carthage lost Sicily and the western part of the island became the first Roman province overseas. The eastern part remained under the rule of Hieron II of Syracuse until his death (215 BC). Carthage was also condemned to pay a war indemnity of 3,200 Euboian talents, 1,000 payable immediately, the balance over ten years (Polybios 1.63.1–3, cf. 62.8–9, Zonaras 8.17) – the equivalent of more than 80 tons of silver. It was a chastening blow, and the future of Carthage seemed reduced to that of a second-rate power.

Remains of the Punic wall of Lilybaeum, Bastione del Fossata Punica, Marsala. In 250 BC the Romans invested and besieged Lilybaeum, one of the two remaining Punic strongholds on Sicily. Despite great improvements in Roman technical skills since Agrigentum, Lilybaeum was to remain in Carthaginian hands until the end of the war. (Author's collection)

Site of the engagement off the Carthaginian naval base at Drepana (249 BC), looking south-west from Torre di Ligny, Trapani. Drepana was the one major sea battle that the Punic Navy won during the war. It was in these waters that the Carthaginian admiral, Adherbal, outmanoeuvred and trapped P. Claudius Pulcher. (Author's collection)

Roman military organization

With the abandonment of the Greek phalanx the Romans adopted the manipular legion, either just before or during their wars with the Samnites (Livy 8.8.3, Sallust *Bellum Catilinae* 51.38). Livy goes so far as to suggest that the phalanx was abandoned after the war with the neighbouring Etruscan city of Veii, that is, at the turn of the 4th century BC, whereas Diodoros (14.16.5, cf. Livy 4.59.11) only refers to the introduction of annual pay to the citizen soldiers at this time. Whatever, despite being tactically more flexible the early legion retained many of the aspects of the hoplite phalanx from which it developed. Thus the Roman Army of our period remained a provisional militia, and the census recorded those citizens with sufficient property to make them eligible to serve the state.

Originally the term *legio* – legion – had meant levy, and obviously referred to the entire citizen force raised by Rome in one year. However, as the number of citizens regularly enrolled for military service increased, the legion became the most important subdivision of the army. By our period the legion consisted of five elements – namely the heavy infantry *hastati*, *principes* and *triarii*, the light infantry *velites*, and the cavalry *equites* – each equipped differently and having specific places in the legion's tactical formation. Its principal strength was the 30 maniples of its heavy infantry, the *velites* and *equites* acting in support of these. These tactical units were deployed in three successive, relatively shallow lines of ten maniples each. It was a force designed for large-scale battles, for standing in the open, moving straightforwardly and smashing its way frontally through any opposition.

We have two accounts of the manipular legion's organization. First, the Roman historian Livy (b. 59 BC), writing more than three centuries after the event, describes the legion of the mid-4th century BC. Second, the Greek historian Polybios, living and writing in Rome at the time, describes the legion of the mid-2nd century BC. The transition between the Livian and Polybian legion is somewhat obscure, but it is clear that some the details Polybios describes apply to the legions of the Hannibalic War.

The Livian legion

In his account of the year 340 BC, after the close of the First Samnite War and as a preamble to the conflict against Rome's erstwhile Latin allies, Livy (8.8.3–8) offers a brief description of Roman military organization. Introduced as part of the Servian reforms, the legions had formerly operated and fought Greek-style in a hoplite phalanx. More recently, however, the Romans had adopted manipular tactics, whereby the legions were now split into distinct battle lines. Behind a screen of lightly armed troops (*leves*) the first line contained maniples (*manipuli*) of *hastati* ('spearmen'), the second line was made up of maniples of *principes* ('chief men') and the third line, made up of the oldest and more mature men, consisted of maniples of *triarii* ('third-rank men'). One significant problem with Livy's account, however, is the fact that he has 15 maniples in each of the three lines as opposed to Polybios' ten maniples (Greek *speírai*). Other groups, whom Livy calls *rorarii* and *accensi*, were lightly equipped and formed a final reserve in the rear, and it is from the definitions compiled by Varro (*De Lingua Latina* 7.57–58) that we can identify the *rorarii* as lightly armed troops and, here he cites the lost *De Re Militari* of Cato the Censor, the *accensi* as military servants.

Despite its anomalies, Livy's account is pleasingly close to that given by Polybios and almost certainly derives from it. Its independent value, therefore,

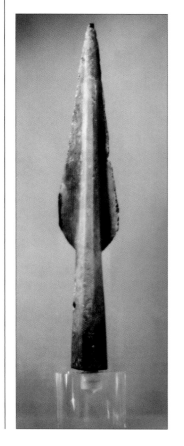

The wealthiest citizen-soldiers of early Rome stood in the foremost ranks of the phalanx and wielded the *doru* and *kopis* of the hoplite. This Etruscan bronze spearhead (Arezzo, Museo Archeologico Nazionale), 5th century BC, once formed the business end of a *doru*, or long thrusting spear. (Esther Carré)

Italic Negau helmet and Graeco-Etruscan greave from Brisighella, Ravenna (San Martino Tomb 10). Albeit Umbrian in context, such equipment would not look out of place in the Greek-style phalanx of early Rome. This type of helmet remained in use unchanged down to the 4th century BC. (Esther Carré)

is not great and, if we choose to accept the evidence of Dionysios of Halikarnassos, he places the manipular system too far back in time. For Dionysios says (20.11) the heavy 'cavalry spear', that is to say the long thrusting-spear of the hoplite, was still employed in battle by the *principes* during the Pyrrhic War (280–275 BC). It seems, therefore, that the transformation from hoplite phalanx to manipular legion was a slow and gradual one, which for Livy (8.8) was a thing over and done with by the early 4th century BC. For the organization of the legion, *terra firma* is reached only with Polybios himself.

The Polybian legion

Polybios breaks off his narrative of the Second Punic War at the nadir of Rome's fortunes, following the three defeats of the Trebbia, Trasimene and Cannae, and turns to an extended digression on the Roman constitution (6.11–18) and army (6.19–42). For us the account of the latter is of inestimable value. Not least in that a contemporary writes the detailed description, himself a former cavalry commander (*hipparchos*) in the Achaian League, who had seen the Roman Army in action against his fellow-countrymen during the Third Macedonian War (171–167 BC) and had perhaps observed its levying and training during his internment in Rome (167–150 BC).

All citizens between 17 and 46 years of age who satisfied the property criteria, namely those who owned property above the value of 11,000 *asses*,[3] were required by the Senate to attend a selection process (*dilectus*) on the Capitol. Although Polybios' passage (6.19.2) is slightly defective here, citizens were liable for 16 years' service as a legionary and ten years for an *eques*. These figures represent the maximum that a man could be called upon to serve. In the 2nd century BC a man was normally expected to serve up to six years in a continuous posting, after which he expected to be released from his military oath. Thereafter he was liable for call-out, as an *evocatus*, up to the maximum of 16 campaigns or years. Some men might serve for a single year at a time, and be obliged to come forward again at the next *dilectus*, until their full six-year period was completed.

---

3 By Polybios' day the minimum property qualification had been fixed at the lower figure of 400 *drachmae* (c.4,000 *asses*), a drastic reduction that can be dated to around 215 BC and attributed to the catastrophic losses inflicted on the army by Hannibal. The following year Rome had considerable difficulty in manning its navy (Livy 24.11.7–9), and this may have been due to the lowering of the qualification for legionary service reducing the number of *proletarii*, who, as Polybios (6.19.3) makes clear, were liable for naval service.

Rome's citizen-militia was organized into legions (*legiones*), usually with a paper-strength of 4,200 legionaries and 300 *equites*. Six military tribunes (*tribuni militum*) were attached to each legion (*legio*), there being no legionary officer with a regular rank in overall command. A *legio* was tactically divided into three lines (*triplex acies*), the legionaries in each being called – from front to rear – *hastati*, *principes* and *triarii*, with the *velites* being normally flung out in front of the *hastati* at the outset of battle, and the *equites* detached to operate on the wings.

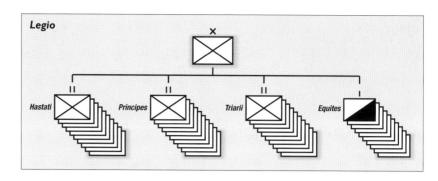

Legio

| Hastati | Principes | Triarii | Equites |

At the *dilectus* the citizen-volunteers were arranged by height and age into some semblance of soldierly order. They were then brought forward four at a time to be selected for service in one of the four consular legions being raised that year. The junior tribunes of each legion took it in turns to have first choice, thus ensuring an even distribution of experience and quality throughout the four units. The new recruits then swore an oath of obedience (*sacramentum dicere*), linking them in a special way with the state, their commander and their fellow citizen-soldiers. This military oath developed over time, apparently being formalized only in 216 BC just before the battle of Cannae, presumably in response to the disasters at the Trebbia and Trasimene when morale had reached rock bottom and a formal oath was seen as a way of remedying this. According to Livy this formal oath took the following form: 'Never to leave the ranks because of fear or to run away, but only to retrieve or grab a weapon, to kill an enemy or to rescue a comrade' (22.38.2–5, cf. Polybios 6.21.1–2). So as to speed up the process it was sworn in full by one man, with the phrase *idem in me* – 'the same for me' – being sufficient for the rest. They were given a date and muster point, and then dismissed to their homes (Polybios 6.26.1–2).

Funerary painting from Paestum (Andriuolo Tomb 86, 330/320 BC) depicting a Samnite warrior returning victorious from battle. Rome was engaged in a tough series of struggles against these people, but eventually absorbed them and converted them into allies, who supplied troops to fight in its wars. (Author's collection)

Heavy infantry

The Romans took great pride in their ability to learn from their enemies, copying weaponry (and tactics) from successive opponents and often improving upon them. This was one of their strong points and, as Polybios rightly says, 'no people are more willing to adopt new customs and to emulate what they see is better done by others' (6.25.10).

The *hastati* and *principes* carried the Italic oval *scutum*, the famous short Iberian sword (*gladius Hispaniensis*), and two sorts of *pila*, heavy and light. The *triarii* were similarly equipped, except they carried a long thrusting-spear (*hasta*) instead of the *pilum* (Polybios 6.23.6). This 2m weapon survives from the era when the Roman army was a hoplite force. The *hasta* was perhaps obsolete in Polybios' day, though probably still in use during the Gallic *tumultus* of 223 BC, when they are, for the only time, mentioned in action (Polybios 2.33.4), while the annalistic tradition does not notice them at all.

In the Livian legion there is no reference to the *pilum*, which, if Livy's account is accepted, may not yet have been introduced. The earliest reference to the *pilum* belongs to 293 BC during the Third Samnite War (Livy 10.39.12, cf. Plutarch *Pyrrhos* 21.9), though the earliest authentic use of this weapon may belong to 251 BC (Polybios 1.40.12). The *pilum* was probably adopted from Iberian mercenaries fighting for Carthage in the First Punic War.

Polybios (6.23.9–11) distinguishes two types of *pilum* (*hyssos* in his Greek), 'thick' and 'thin', saying each man had both types. Surviving examples from Numantia (near Burgos, Spain), the site of a Roman siege (134–133 BC), confirm two basics types of construction. Both have a small pyramid-shaped point at the end of a narrow soft-iron shank, fitted to a wooden shaft some 1.4m in length. One type has the shank socketed, while the other has a wide flat iron tang riveted to a thickened section of the wooden shaft. The last type is probably Polybios' 'thick' *pilum*, referring to the broad joint of iron and wood. This broad section can be either square of round in section, and is strengthened by a small iron ferrule. The iron shank varies in length, with many examples averaging around 70cm.

All of the weapon's weight was concentrated behind the small pyramidal tip, giving it great penetrative power. The length of the iron shank gave it the reach to punch through an enemy's shield and still go on to wound his body, but even if it failed to do so and merely stuck in the shield it was very difficult to pull free and might force the man to discard his weighted-down shield and fight unprotected. A useful side effect of this 'armour-piercing' weapon was that the narrow shank would often bend on impact, ensuring that the enemy would not throw it back. The maximum range of the *pilum* was some 30m, but its effective range something like half that. Throwing a *pilum* at close range would have improved both accuracy and armour penetration.

A later lexicographer, possibly following Polybios' lost account of the Iberian War (fr. 179), says the *gladius Hispaniensis* was adopted from the Iberians (or Celtiberi[4]) at the time of the Hannibalic War, but it is possible that this weapon, along with the *pilum*, was adopted from Iberian mercenaries serving Carthage during the First Punic War. It was certainly in use by 197 BC, when Livy (31.34.4) describes the Macedonians' shock at the terrible wounds it inflicted.

The Iberians used a short, but deadly sword. This was either the *falcata*, a curved single-bladed weapon derived from the Greek *kopis*, or the cut-and-thrust sword, a straight-bladed weapon from which the *gladius* was derived (Polybios 3.114.2–4, Livy 22.46.6). The earliest Roman specimens date to the turn of the 1st century BC ('Mainz' type), but a 4th-century sword of similar shape has been found in Spain at the cemetery of Los Cogotes (Avila). The Roman blade could be as much as 64 to 69cm in length and 4.8 to 6cm wide and waisted in the centre. It was a fine piece of 'blister steel' with a triangular point between 9.6 and 20cm long and honed-down razor-sharp edges, and was designed to puncture armour. It had a comfortable bone handgrip grooved to fit the fingers, and a large spherical pommel, usually of wood or ivory, to help with counter-balance. Extant examples weigh between 1.2 and 1.6kg.

The legionary also carried a dagger, *pugio*. The dagger – a short, edged, stabbing weapon – was the ultimate weapon of last resort. However, it was probably more often employed in the day-to-day tasks of living on campaign. Like the *gladius*, the Roman dagger was borrowed from the Iberians and then developed.

Polybios says (6.23.14–15) all soldiers wore a bronze pectoral, a span (23cm) square, to protect the heart and chest, although those who could afford it would wear instead an iron mail shirt (*lorica hamata*). He also adds that a bronze helmet was worn, without describing it, but the Attic, Montefortino and Etrusco-Corinthian styles were all popular in Italy at this time and were probably all used, as they certainly all were by later Roman troops. He does say (6.23.12–13) helmets were crested with a circlet of feathers and three upright black or crimson feathers a cubit (46cm) tall, so exaggerating the wearer's height. Interestingly, Polybios (6.23.8) clearly refers to only one greave being worn, and Arrian (*Taktika* 3.5), writing more or less three centuries later, confirms this, saying the ancient Romans used to wear one greave only, on the leading leg, the left. No doubt many of those who could afford it would actually have a pair of bronze greaves covering the leg from ankle to knee.

To complete his defensive equipment, each soldier carried a body shield (*scutum*). Polybios (6.23.2–5) describes the *scutum* in detail, and his account is confirmed by the remarkable discovery of a shield of this type at Kasr-el-Harit in the Fayûm, Egypt. The *scutum* was oval in shape, some 1.2m in length and 60cm in width and constructed from three layers of birch plywood, each laid at right angles to the next, and covered with canvas and then calfskin. It was thicker in the centre and flexible at the edges, making it very resilient to blows, and the top and bottom edges were reinforced with bronze or iron edging to prevent splitting. Nailed to the front and running vertically from top to bottom was a wooden spine (*spina*). Good protection came at a price, for the *scutum* was heavy, around 10kg, and in battle its entire weight was borne by the left arm as the soldier held the horizontal handgrip behind the bronze or iron boss (*umbo*), which reinforced the central spine of the shield. The *scutum* is clearly recognizable on the Altar of Domitius Ahenobarbus.

Finally, lest we forget, these short-term citizen-soldiers provided their own equipment and therefore we should expect considerably more variation in clothing, armour and weapons than the legionaries of the later professional Imperial legions.

---

4 An influx of Gauls had earlier mingled with the indigenous Iberian inhabitants to form an essentially tribal society of natural horsemen and warriors, moody, emotional, and quick to see insult.

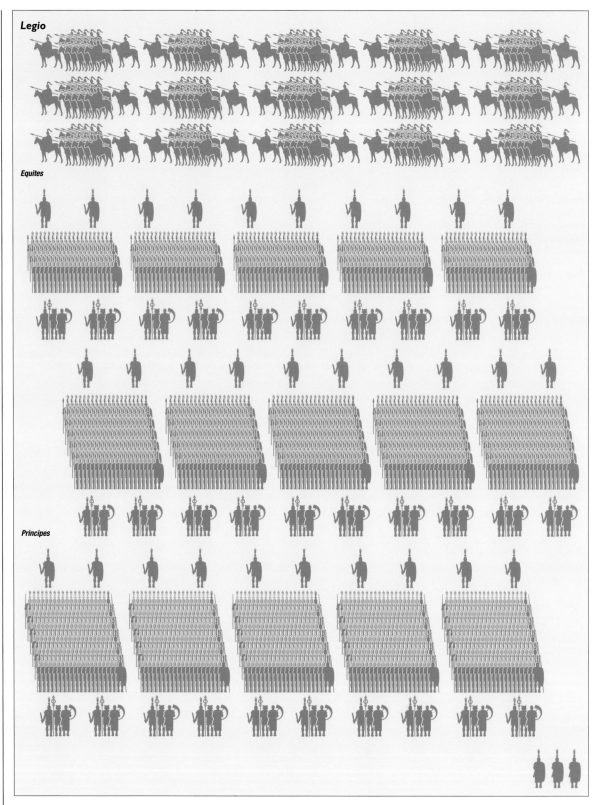

Legio

Equites

Principes

A *legio*, mustering a nominal strength of 4,200 legionaries with 300 *equites* attached, routinely deployed in three lines – four including the *velites* skirmishing in front – the ten *manipuli* of each side by side, but with gaps between them corresponding to the width of a *manipulus*. The *hastati* form the first line, their ten *manipuli* deployed with intervals between them. The ten *manipuli* of the *principes* in the

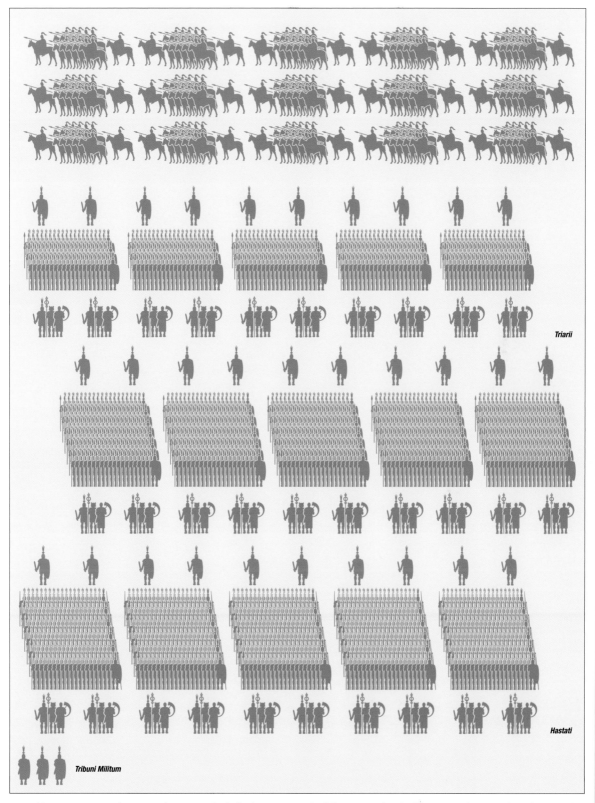

Triarii

Hastati

Tribuni Militum

second line are positioned to cover these gaps. Similarly, the ten *manipuli* of the *triarii* in the third line cover the intervals in the second. We have no direct evidence for the distance between the three lines. At the front of the entire formation are the six military tribunes (*tribuni militum*).

Maniple

Originally the term *manipulus* meant 'a handful'. Then, as in the early days a pole with a handful of hay twisted round it was used as a standard, *manipulus* came to signify this, and hence a unit of soldiers belonging to the same standard. The legion itself consisted of 1,200 *hastati* in ten maniples of 120, 1,200 *principes* organized in the same way, and 600 *triarii* also in ten maniples.

The tactical subunit was the maniple (*manipulus*), of which there were 30 per *legio*, ten for each of the lines with the *velites* equally distributed among them for organization purposes. A *manipulus* had a nominal strength of either 120 (*hastati*, *principes*) or 60 legionaries (*triarii*). For administrative purposes only, each *manipulus* was split into two centuries (*centuriae*), giving a total of 60 *manipuli* per *legio*.

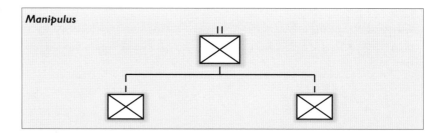

Manipulus

Legionaries on the Altar of Domitius Ahenobarbus (Paris, musée du Louvre, Ma 975) equipped with the arms and armour of the last two centuries of the Republic. Each wears an Etrusco-Corinthian helmet and mail armour, and carries an oval *scutum* constructed of plywood, canvas and calfskin. (Author's collection)

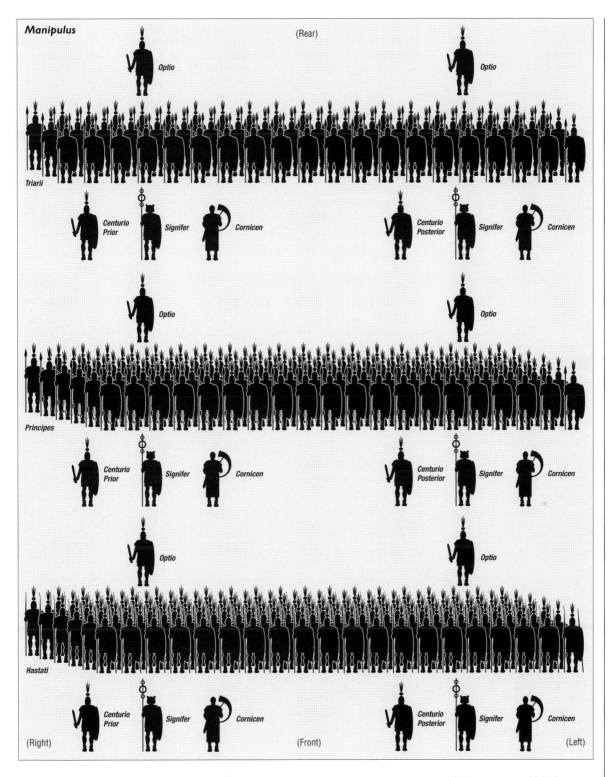

Manipulus

(Rear)

Optio / Optio

Triarii

Centurio Prior / Signifer / Cornicen / Centurio Posterior / Signifer / Cornicen

Optio / Optio

Principes

Centurio Prior / Signifer / Cornicen / Centurio Posterior / Signifer / Cornicen

Optio / Optio

Hastati

Centurio Prior / Signifer / Cornicen / Centurio Posterior / Signifer / Cornicen

(Right) (Front) (Left)

Whereas both *hastati* and *principes* normally had 120 legionaries to a *manipulus*, the *triarii* mustered only 60. A *manipulus* would deploy six (*hastati, principes*) or three (*triarii*) deep, and in order to give each man room to use his weapons he would have, if we are to believe Polybios (18.30.5–8), a frontage of six Roman feet (1.8m) as well as an equivalent depth. On the other hand, Vegetius (3.14, 15), who appears to be using Cato the Censor as his source here, claims the individual legionaries occupy a frontage of three Roman feet (0.9m) with a depth of six Roman feet (1.8m) between ranks. This close-order formation gives a *manipulus* a frontage of approximately 18m and a depth of 12m (*hastati, principes*) or 6m (*triarii*). In these examples, the *manipuli* are drawn up with their respective centuries (*centuriae*) side by side.

The *velites* were armed with a sword, the *gladius Hispaniensis* according to Livy (38.21.15), and a bundle of javelins, with long thin iron heads a span (23cm) in length, which bent at the first impact. For protection they wore a helmet without a crest and carried a round shield (*parma*) but wore no armour. In order to be distinguished from a distance, some *velites* would cover their plain helmets with a wolf's skin or something similar (Polybios 6.22.1–3). As for the number of javelins carried, Polybios does not specify. Livy, on the other hand, says (26.4.4) *velites* had seven javelins apiece, whilst the 2nd-century Roman poet Lucilius (7.290) has them carrying five each.

According to Livy, the *hastati* were also men in the flower of youth, the *principes* in the prime of manhood and the *triarii* seasoned veterans. The same order for the three lines appears in Polybios' narrative (14.8.5, 15.9.7), and in Livy's also (30.8.5, 32.11, 34.10) as well as in other antiquarian sources (Varro *De Lingua Latina* 5.89, Ovid *Fasti* 3.128–132), and is implied by the order of seniority among centurions of the imperial army where *pilus* was the most senior followed by the *princeps* and then the *hastatus*.[5]

Polybios (2.24.13, 6.20.9) puts the nominal strength of a legion at 4,200 legionaries. However, in times of particular crisis when larger legions were raised, as was the case at Cannae, this might be increased to as many as 5,000. Polybios says (6.21.9–10) when this happened the number of *triarii* remained the same at 600, but the number of *hastati*, *principes* (and *velites*), the less experienced legionaries, increased from the usual 1,200. As a result, the size of a maniple of *hastati* or *principes* could increase from 120 to 160 men when the legion was first formed and before any campaign losses had occurred.

Light infantry

Of the 4,200 legionaries in a legion, 3,000 were heavy infantry. The remaining 1,200 men, the youngest and poorest, served as light infantry and were known as *velites* or 'cloak-wearers', that is, they lacked any body armour. However, it is important to remember that the distinction between what Greek and Roman sources call 'heavy' and 'light' infantry, was not so much that the latter were more lightly equipped than the former, but that heavy infantry were trained to fight together in formation, whereas light infantry were trained to fight as skirmishers.

According to Livy (26.4.9), the *velites* were formally created as a force in 211 BC, leading to suggestions that they replayed the less well-armed and efficient *leves* (or *rorarii*). However, this single passage in Livy is fraught with problems, and he (21.55.11) does mention them at the Trebbia in 218 BC. It is more likely that the terms were synonymous, although perhaps *velites* came into common usage at a later period.

Light infantry were divided for administrative purpose among the heavy infantry of the maniples, each maniple being allocated the same number of *velites* (Polybios 6.21.7, 24.4). As for the *hastati* and *principes*, at times of crisis the number of *velites* might be increased.

Cavalry

Each legion had a small cavalry force of 300 organized in ten *turmae* (Greek *ilai*) of 30 troopers each (Polybios 6.20.8–9, 25.1, cf. 2.24.13, Livy 3.62). The military tribunes appointed three *decuriones* (Greek *ilarchai*) to each *turma*, of whom the senior commanded with the rank of *praefectus*. Each *decurio* chose an *optio* (Greek *ouragos*) as his second-in-command and rear-rank officer (Polybios 6.25.1–2). This organization suggests that the *turma* was divided into three files of ten, each led by a *decurio* ('leader of ten') and closed by an *optio*. These files were clearly not independent tactical subunits, for the *turma* was evidently intended to operate as a single entity, as indicated by the seniority of one *decurio* over his two colleagues.

The cavalry, or *equites*, formed the most prestigious element of the legion, and were recruited from the wealthiest citizens able to afford a horse and its trappings (Polybios 6.20.9). By our period these included the top 18 centuries (*centuriae*) of the voting assembly, the *comitia centuriata*, who were rated *equites equo publico*, the equestrian elite, obliging the state to provide them with the cost of a remount should their horse be killed on active service. M. Porcius Cato (cos. 195 BC) was later to boast that his grandfather had had five horses killed under him in battle and replaced by the state (Plutarch *Cato*

---

5 Cf. Vegetius 2.2, 15–17, 3.14, where he places the *principes* in the front line, then the *hastati*, while the *triarii* are armed like the other two lines with *pila*. In his defence, however, he does say (1.8) that he used Cato the Censor as a source.

Turma

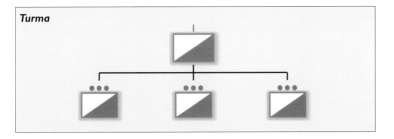

Attached to each *legio* was a small cavalry detachment some 300 strong and divided into ten tactical subunits known as *turmae*. With a nominal strength of 30 troopers, each *turma* was organized, probably for administrative purposes only, as three smaller subunits, each one commanded by a *decurio* with an *optio* acting as his second-in-command. The senior of the three *decuriones* also held overall responsibility for the *turma* as a whole.

Turma

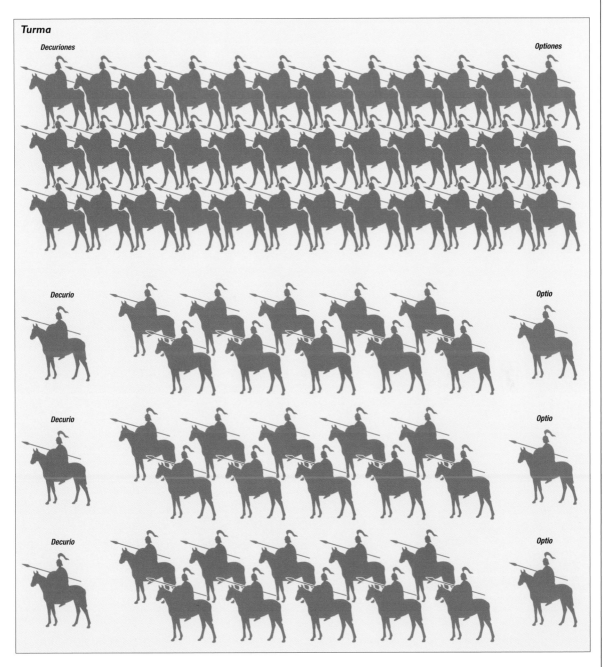

The *turma* is divided into three files of ten troopers, each led by a *decurio* ('leader of ten') and closed by an *optio*. Alternatively, and depending on the circumstances, the *turma* can deploy in six rows of five. The first selected *decurio* commands the unit as a whole.

Cavalry

Polybios (6.25.3–8) discusses the changes in the Roman cavalry in some detail, emphasizing that the *equites* were now armed in 'the Greek fashion', namely bronze helmet, linen corselet, strong circular shield, long spear, complete with a butt-spike, and sword, but he observes that formerly (perhaps up to the Pyrrhic War) they had lacked body armour and had carried only a short thrusting-spear and a small ox-hide shield, which was too light for adequate protection at close quarters and tended to rot in the rain. Polybios actually compares its shape to a type of round-bossed cake, namely those that are commonly used in sacrifices. This earlier shield may be the type shown on the Tarentine 'horsemen' coins of the early 4th century BC, with a flat rim and convex centre. For what it is worth, Livy mentions 'little round cavalry shields' (2.20.10, cf. 4.28) in use as early as 499 BC.

Intriguingly the sword now carried by the *equites* appears to have been the *gladius Hispaniensis*, for when Livy (31.34.1–5) describes the horror felt by Macedonian troops on seeing the hideous wounds inflicted upon their comrades, the perpetrators were Roman cavalrymen. If true, then the *gladius* used by the *equites* may well have been a little longer than that of the infantry. Livy refers to 'arms torn away, shoulders and all, heads separated from bodies with the necks completely severed, and stomachs ripped open' (31.34.4).

Contrary to popular belief, the lack of stirrups was not a major handicap to ancient horsemen, especially those 'born in the saddle'. Moreover, Roman cavalry of the time were perhaps already using the Celtic four-horned saddle, which provided an admirably firm seat. When a rider's weight was lowered onto this type of saddle the four tall horns (*corniculae*) closed around and gripped his thighs, but they did not inhibit free movement to the same extent as a modern pommel and cantle designed for rider comfort and safety. This was especially important to spear-armed horsemen, whose drill called for some almost acrobatic changes of position.

While aristocratic horsemen (*equites*) served in the army, the Romans did not have a tradition of horsemanship. Most of the cavalry, therefore, were provided for by the Latin/Italian *socii*. Limestone cinerary urn (Cortona, Museo dell' Accademia Etrusca) with a relief of an Etruscan horseman fighting two Gauls. (Author's collection)

the Censor 1). Being young aristocrats, the *equites* were enthusiastic and brave, but better at making a headlong charge on the battlefield than patrolling or scouting. This was a reflection of the lack of a real cavalry tradition in Rome, as well as the fact that the *equites* included the sons of many senators, eager

to make a name for courage and so help their future political careers. Before being eligible for political office in Rome a man had to have served for ten campaigns with the army.

Citizen-militia

It is important to note that the legions in this period were not the long-lived institutions of the later professional army and appear to have been re-numbered each year. It is extremely rare for our sources to explain in detail when legions were raised, disbanded, destroyed or incorporated into other units. The weakness of the consular system was that every time the legions were discharged and a new army raised, the whole process had to start again from scratch. Few units would have developed a lasting sense of *esprit de corps* or identity.

Taking the Polybian *drachma* as the equivalent of the *denarius*, the legionary received an allowance (*stipendium*) of one *denarius* every three days (120 *denarii* per annum), the payment going towards the cost of his rations, clothes and extra equipment. Centurions received double that rate, while the *equites* received even more, one *denarius* per diem, from which to meet the cost of maintaining their mounts (Polybios 6.39.12, 15). Miserly as it was, the actual amount of money was not meant to be a substitute for normal living expenses. It was well below the wages of an unskilled labourer, who commanded about 12 *asses* per diem (432 *denarii* per annum) in this period. But merely counting how many *asses* soldiers receive misses the point. Roman society had never been broken into the three Indo-European categories, often hereditary, of military, religious and economic groups, as was common in similar civilizations. Thus throughout the republican period the soldiers fighting for Rome were its own citizens for whom defence of the state was regarded, by the Senate at least, as a duty, a responsibility and a privilege.

When a man came forward voluntarily, he would presumably be accepted gladly, unless, of course, the volunteer was too old, too unfit, or just under-aged. But there was always a measure of compulsion, and in a loose sense service in the legions of the middle Republic can be likened to 'national service' in many Western democracies in the mid-20th century: an obligation on every fit male as his contribution to a country's defence. At first, service in the Roman Army entailed a citizen being away from his home – usually a farmstead – for a few weeks or months over the summer. But the need to fight overseas in Iberia and to leave troops to form permanent garrisons in the newly won provinces of Sicily and Sardinia meant that men were away from home for longer periods. This interruption from normal life could easily spell ruin to the soldier-farmers who had traditionally made up the bulk of citizens eligible for military call-up. Hopkins (1978: 35) estimates that in 225 BC legionaries comprised 17 per cent of all the adult male citizens, and in 213 BC, at the height of the Second Punic War, 29 per cent. Inevitably what had been seen as a duty and voluntary obligation took on a somewhat different character.

Socii military organization

Based on a Celtic design, the Montefortino helmet was basically a hemispherical bowl beaten to shape, with a narrow peaked neck-guard and an integral crest knob. Such helmets also frequently had large, scalloped cheek-pieces. This 4th-century example (Volterra, Museo Guarnacci, V 54) comes from an Etruscan burial. (Esther Carré)

As well as citizens, Rome called on allied troops, at first from its Latin neighbours and then from all Italy. Essentially, when they painfully struggled to obtain the mastery of the peninsula, the Romans had two codes of dealing with peoples who opposed them. If the enemy resisted them outright, so that the Romans had to take the city by storm, then the whole community might be enslaved and their city destroyed. But if they submitted to the commander of the besieging force in good time – normally before the first siege machines had been brought against their walls – then a different custom prevailed, that is to say they were expected to surrender unconditionally. Having done so, according to Roman law, the enemy were now said to have made a *deditio*. At this juncture the enemy were classed as *dediticii*, having, as it was said publicly, 'sought the protection of the honour of the Roman people' (*in fidem populi Romani se dedere*). They now had to await the decision of the Senate on their fate.

The Senate, in the light of experience acquired from many struggles and difficulties, would invariably choose the better course of action and bind the Latin and Italian communities to Rome by a long series of bilateral treaties, a multi-tiered system of control that respected the time-honoured principle of *divide et impera*.[6] These treaties normally specified that an allied community must contribute a specific number of troops, as determined by the Roman people (*populus Romanus*), to aid the Romans in times of war, and in return allowed them a share in any booty. Otherwise the ally paid no tribute to Rome and remained free to pursue its own cultural agenda. The durability of the arrangement is famous, and here we should note the great difficulty that Hannibal had in detaching Rome's allies in Italy. The precise obligations of the community under the treaty varied according to the conditions in which the treaty was made. A few were entirely voluntary agreements, but most were compulsory, resulting from a *deditio* in time of war.

The allies (*socii*) were divided into two broad groups: Latins and Italians. The *socii nominis Latini*, 'allies of the Latin name', included a handful of old communities that had not been granted citizenship after Rome's defeat of its insurgent allies in 338 BC, as well as 30 Latin colonies, such as Placentia (Piacenza), Cremona and Brundisium strategically sited throughout Italy. Their main duty was to supply troops to Rome, these communities being capable of producing 80,000 infantry and 5,000 cavalry between them according to Polybios (2.24), and the greater part of the army was either Roman or Latin. The

---

6 Rome was unique in the ancient world in its willingness to grant citizenship to outsiders and make them loyal to it. Some former enemies became citizens with full rights (*optimo iure*) or citizens with limited rights, namely 'citizens without the vote' (*civitas sine suffragio*), whilst others were granted the lesser rights of Latins, but allowed the rights of intermarriage and commerce with Roman citizens, each grade being a legal status, rather than reflecting actual ethnic or linguistic distinctions.

other allies were Italians of various nations – in the same passage Polybios mentions Sabini and Etruscans from central Italy, Umbri and Sarsinati from the Apennines, Veneti and Cenomani from Gallia Cisalpina, Iapygii and Messapii from Apulia, and Samnites, Lucani, Marsi, Marrucini, Frentani and Vestini from the southern Apennines – and could provide a further 260,000 infantry and 34,000 cavalry. All allies were theoretically obliged to help Rome with their total manpower, but in practice their obligations may have been defined by what was known as the *formula togatorum*, 'list of adult males', a kind of sliding scale requiring so many men for the number of citizen-soldiers raised in any year (Brunt 1971: 545–48).

Many of the Latin colonists were in fact descended from Roman citizens, men who had accepted Latin status in place of Roman citizenship in order to make a fresh start (Livy 27.9.10–11). Thus the culture of these colonies was virtually identical to that of Rome, with the same gods, similar institutions and certain rights in Roman law. On the other hand, Rome's Italian allies were a diverse lot, being politically, geographically, ethnically, culturally and often linguistically distinct. They were in theory independent, although in practice Rome was clearly the dominant partner in the alliances. The Senate's capability to intervene in the dealings of the *socii* arose out of its role in foreign affairs, and in particular its duty to secure the confederation and ensure the supremacy of Rome.

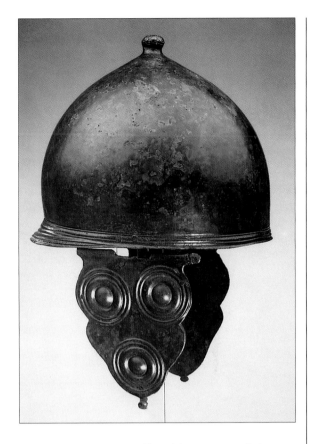

Ala

A Latin or Italian *ala*, wing, accompanied each Roman legion, theoretically with the same number of allied infantry as citizen infantry, along with three times as many allied cavalry as citizen cavalry (Polybios 6.26.7–8). In practice there were often more allies than Romans – 20,000 allied infantry to 16,000 Roman legionaries at the Trebbia for example (Polybios 3.72.11, cf. Livy 21.55.4). Roman officers called *praefecti sociorum*, apparently three to an *ala*, commanded the allies (Polybios 6.26.5). Appointed by the consuls, the prefects' role was probably similar to that of the military tribunes in a legion. At lower levels the allies evidently provided their own officers – we know the name of the commander of the soldiers from Praeneste at Casilinum, Marcus Anicius (Livy 23.17.11).

One of the commonest designs throughout Italy, the Montefortino helmet offered good defence from downward blows. Large cheek-pieces protected the face without obscuring the wearer's vision or hearing, and those of this 3rd-century Samnite example (Karlsruhe, Badisches Landesmuseum, AG 197) are identical in design to the triple-disc cuirass. (Esther Carré)

Rome's Latin and Italian allies (*socii*) were organized into *alae*. Each one had roughly the same number of infantry as a *legio*, but twice as many cavalry after deducting the one-third serving as *extraordinarii*. These were probably organized as 20 *turmae*. Though the infantry camped in *manipuli*, the *cohors* was the tactical subunit of an *ala*, ten *cohortes* drawn from several allied communities being brigaded to form the unit with two being earmarked to serve as the *extraordinarii*. Each *ala* was commanded by three prefects (*praefecti sociorum*) who were Roman citizens.

Ala (extraordinarii detached)

× (-)

III   I

The pick of the Latin and Italian allies, one-third of the cavalry and one-fifth of the infantry, were separated from the *alae* to form a detached corps known as the *extraordinarii*. This elite force of cavalry and infantry was placed at the immediate disposal of the consul. In a standard consular army, therefore, four *cohortes* of infantry and 20 *turmae* of cavalry formed the *extraordinarii*. As a rule they were placed at the head of the column, but during a retreat they dropped back and formed the rearguard instead of the advanced guard.

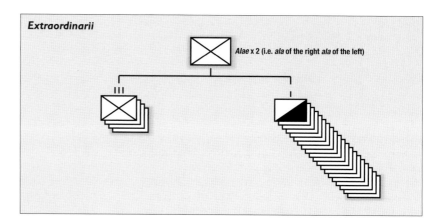

Extraordinarii

Alae x 2 (i.e. *ala* of the right *ala* of the left)

The Etrusco-Corinthian helmet was still in use by legionaries and is associated with the *triarii*. This 5th-century Italic-Greek example (Taranto, Museo Archeologico Nazionale, 73002) is without cheek-pieces, but it still retains the characteristic crest holder. Developed from the Corinthian type, this style preserved the eyeholes for decoration. (Author's collection)

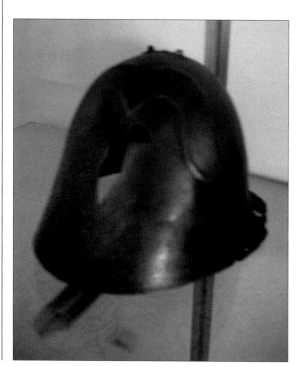

Cohors

An elite force of *extraordinarii* was selected from the best of the allied troops, one-third of the cavalry and one-fifth of the infantry, who camped near the consul's tent (*praetorium*) and were at his immediate disposal. Apart from these picked troops, each allied unit was composed of men from one town, canton or nation, and would take the standard oath before setting out to join the assembled citizen forces under their own commander and paymaster (Polybios 6.21.2).

Although Polybios assumes the infantry camped in *manipuli*, the *cohors* was the standard unit both for recruitment and tactics well before the Romans employed it and at least as early as the Second Punic War. It may originally have been a Samnite unit, so some allies may have used it before their incorporation into the Roman Army. Allied *cohortes* of 460 (Livy 23.17.11), 500 (Livy 23.17.8), and 600 (Livy 28.45.20) men are recorded, and the variance in size probably reflects the differing sizes of each community's population. Maniples probably existed as subunits within the cohort, with 10 cohorts drawn from different communities place together to form an *ala*.

Cavalry

As noted already, the allied cavalry force was generally two or three times larger than that of the citizens. These horsemen were organized in *turmae* of probably the same strength as the Roman, and were presumably also from the wealthiest strata of society. This is certainly suggested by Livy's references (23.7.2, 24.13.1) to 300 young men of the noblest Campanian families serving in Sicily, and to the young noblemen from Tarentum who served at the battles of Trasimene and Cannae. The cavalry were commanded, at least from the 2nd century BC, by Roman *praefecti equitum*, presumably with local *decuriones* and *optiones* at *turma* level. Like their citizen counterparts, as well as having a higher social status, allied horsemen were much better paid than those serving as foot soldiers (Polybios 6.39.14–15).

Command and control

Under the Republic, Rome was rule by pairs of annually elected magistrates called consuls, who abdicated power at the end of the year but held absolute military and civil authority during their term of office. Lesser magistrates were also annual and in pairs, an expedient to allow them to veto each other and thereby prevent the concentration of power in one man's hands, an expedient intended to prevent the emergence of a tyrant or king (*rex*). This principle of collegiality was basic to the Roman constitution.

A council of 300, the Senate, advised the magistrates. Theoretically it had no constitutional powers, its decrees (*Senatus consultum*), passed on a majority vote, were not law but merely consultative. Yet it should be noted that the

Imperium was symbolized by the magistrates' lictors, who carried the *fasces*, axes bound around with a bundle of rods indicating that their master could decree both capital and corporal punishment. Four such badges of office decorate this tombstone (Naples, Museo Archeologico Nazionale) of a former consul. (Author's collection)

Caius Flaminius (d. 217 BC)

Caius Flaminius (cos. I 223 BC, cos. II 217 BC) was a *novus homo*, 'new man', the first in his *gens* to hold Rome's highest magistracy, the consulship, which was usually dominated by a small group of aristocratic *gentes*. Both Polybios (3.80.3–82.8) and Livy (21.63.1–15, 22.3.3–14) portray him as an aggressive demagogue, a man of bold words but little talent who had based his career on pandering to the desires of the poorest citizens.

As for his abilities, while serving as tribune of the plebs (232 BC) he had succeeded in passing a farsighted bill (*plebis scita*) to distribute much of the captured ager Gallicus et Picenus to poorer citizens, as a praetor (227 BC) he had been the first governor of Sicily, and as a censor (220 BC) he had overseen the building of the via Flaminia, the great consular road that ran from Rome to Ariminum (Rimini) and the newly colonized land in the north. Moreover, as consul in 223 BC he had commanded in the field in Gallia Cisalpina with considerable success – yet success against 'barbarians' was no real preparation for facing a commander of Hannibal's calibre.

Having defeated the Insubres and returned triumphant to Rome, it is interesting to note that the people voted Flaminius a triumph in spite of the opposition of most of the Senate (*Fasti Triumphales* 530 AUC). Flaminius' career had certainly been controversial, but it had also been exceptionally distinguished, even by the standards of the period, and especially so for a *novus homo*. It seems the maverick Flaminius had made many enemies, men who would savage his reputation after his tragic death at Trasimene.

word 'Senate', derived from the Latin term for old man (*senex*), reflects the fact that senators were appointed for life. As an advisory council (*consilium*), it discussed a whole gamut of political and religious business, but came to be particularly important in foreign affairs.

The Romans did not maintain a strict division between army and politics, and senators followed a career that brought them both military and civilian responsibilities, sometimes simultaneously. Command was thus assigned to Rome's senior magistrates, the consuls and praetors, each receiving for the duration of his office *imperium*. This was the almost mystical authority to command armies and to dispense justice and, as holders of *imperium*, they could compel absolute obedience except from someone with greater authority, *imperium maius*. What was intrinsically the power of life and death was symbolized by an axe (*securis*) enclosed in a bundle of rods (*fasces*) carried by lictors, their bodyguard attendants – 12 for consuls and six for praetors.

As the chief magistrates, the two consuls provided the commanders for the most important of Rome's conflicts. Although these men owed their election primarily to their social standing rather than to any military ability, they usually led an army each: consular legions were numbered *I* to *IIII*, one consul commanding *legiones I* and *III*, the other *legiones II* and *IIII*. When more than two consular armies were operating, other magistrates, such as praetors, or ex-consuls (proconsuls) and ex-praetors (propraetors), would be pressed into office for the minor commands.

With regards to proconsuls and propraetors, the Senate used the system of prorogation, whereby a man's *imperium* would be renewed for a further term. In a national emergency the whole system could be overridden and a dictator chosen to take supreme command, with a *magister equitum*, 'master of horse', as his subordinate.[7] A semi-regal position, the dictator held double-consular *imperium*, running all military and domestic affairs for the six months he was in office, effectively taking over the running of the state (*rei gerundae causa*); that done, his authority immediately lapsed.

---

7 When the office of dictator had been created in an earlier period, it was considered important that he should fight on foot with the warriors of the phalanx, the yeoman-farmers who were the heart of the military system of the early Republic. So the dictator was prohibited from riding a horse, leaving his deputy to command the cavalry. Such a restriction was no longer appropriate for the task of commanding the much larger and more sophisticated armies of the middle Republic. Despite this, however, with the Romans being obsessed with the culture and traditions of their ancestors (*mos maiorum*), a newly appointed dictator still had to gain special permission from the Senate to ride a horse.

Q. Fabius Maximus Cunctator (d. 203 BC)

In the wake of the disaster at Trasimene Rome appointed a dictator, Q. Fabius Maximus (cos. I 233 BC, cos. II 228 BC, dict. 217 BC, cos. III 215 BC, cos. IV 214 BC, cos. V 209 BC). He was now 58 years of age, rather old for a Roman general, and had served as a youth in the First Punic War, subsequently being twice elected to the consulship. He was to gain the pejorative cognomen 'Cunctator', the Delayer, because, recognizing that he was not able to cope with Hannibal on the field of battle, he wisely chose to conduct a campaign of delays and small war, the one thing Hannibal could not afford, but also the one thing the Romans could not tolerate or understand. His officers and soldiers nicknamed him 'Hannibal's *paedogogus*' after the slave who followed a Roman schoolboy carrying his books (Plutarch *Fabius Maximus* 5).

There can be little doubt, by exercising the privilege of hindsight, that at this time Fabius' strategy of caution and delay was the correct one, and that his appointment prevented yet another consular army being served up to meet its almost inevitable doom at Hannibal's hands in 217 BC. As Polybios sagely remarks (3.89.8–9), in refusing to be drawn into pitched battles, Fabius was falling back on factors in which Rome had the advantage, namely inexhaustible supplies of men and *matériel*.

But it was bound to be unpopular and unspectacular, and it was to prove extremely costly to the Italian countryside, particularly in the rich ager Falernus (Polybios 3.90.7–92.10, Livy 22.13.1–15.1). All credit must be given to Fabius for the iron self-will that he exhibited in the face of a steadily growing public outcry against his methods. And the constant bickering, disloyalty and downright disobedience of his *magister equitum* M. Minucius Rufus (cos. 221 BC), who wanted to throw Fabius' strategy overboard and attack Hannibal, made a difficult situation worse. He certainly deserved the tribute paid him by the contemporary poet, Ennius, who described him as 'the man who on his own by delaying (*cunctando*) restored the situation for us', a line that received the accolade of being immortalized by Virgil (*Aeneid* 6.846).

Unfortunately the two consuls or the dictator and his lieutenant could often be personal or political rivals, which did not help unity of command. Another weakness with this system was that they would all have some military experience, but often no experience of command, and they were not always chosen for their generalship. To be frank, they often displayed a conspicuous lack of it and Roman armies frequently had to win despite their senatorial generals. In a remarkable passage drawn from Cassius Dio, Zonaras, an early 12th-century Byzantine monk, goes so far as to claim that the greatest mistake the earlier Romans made was to send out different commanders each year, depriving them of command just as they were learning the art of generalship, 'as though choosing them for practice, not use' (8.16).

Legion command

The legion had no overall commander, being officered by six military tribunes (*tribuni militum*) drawn from the senatorial aristocracy. Like all senior officers of the army, these men were not professional soldiers but magistrates elected by the citizens in the *comitia centuriata*. Having served a five-year military apprenticeship – young aristocrats almost certainly fulfilled this obligation serving in the cavalry – they would be eligible for election to the rank of military tribune, although ten of the 24 annually elected tribunes needed to have at least ten years' service experience (Polybios 6.19.1). If more than four legions were employed in any given year, extra tribunes, nicknamed *Rufuli* ('redheads'), would be appointed, presumably on the grounds of proven ability and experience, by the consuls. By following the conventional *cursus honorum*, or 'course of honours', a rising aristocrat could gain further military experience as a quaestor or a praetor, before eventually reaching the consulship.

The military tribunes were assigned to individual legions. The 14 junior tribunes divided themselves into four groups, according to the order in which the people had appointed them, the four tribunes first appointed being assigned to *legio I*, the next three to *legio II*, the next four to *legio III*, and the last three to *legio IIII*. Of the ten senior tribunes the first two were appointed to *legio I*, the next three to *legio II*, the next two to *legio III*, and the last three to *legio IIII* (Polybios 6.19.9–10).

Having been appointed to their unit the military tribunes had a wide range of responsibilities, both administrative and tactical. Their job was to enrol new recruits, exact the military oath from them and divide their infantry into their four categories. They may have also been responsible for the training of the recruits, as well as their health and general welfare (Polybios 10.20.1). Furthermore, they were responsible for the selection of a suitable campsite and the supervision of the camps, and had the ability to punish, through inflicting fines or ordering floggings, certain offences. Tribunes worked in pairs, each pair commanding the legion for two months out of every six. They drew lots for their turn (Polybios 6.26.9, 34.3, 37.5).

The war-god Mars on the Altar of Domitius Ahenobarbus (Paris, musée du Louvre, Ma 975) dressed in the uniform of a senior officer, most probably that of a military tribune. He wears a muscled cuirass with two rows of fringed *pteruges*, and a crested Etrusco-Corinthian helmet. (Author's collection)

The military tribunes were responsible to the overall commander of the army, one of the two consuls, who would in many cases have only two legions of Roman citizens accompanied by an equal or larger number of *socii*, Latin and Italian allies (Polybios 3.109.12). Smaller-scale operations could be entrusted to praetors, the next magisterial college in seniority to the consuls, who were normally given an army of one legion supported by a similarly sized contingent of allied soldiers. There had been one praetor each year until 242 BC, and in that year a second was added (Livy *Peiochae* 19). Thereafter, they were distinguished as the 'city praetor' (*praetor urbanus*) and the 'foreign praetor' (*praetor peregrinus*).

Legionaries on the Altar of Domitius Ahenobarbus (Paris, musée du Louvre, Ma 975) wearing iron mail shirts, thigh-length with shoulder doubling for extra protection against downward sword strokes. The belt would transfer some of the shirt's weight (c.15kg) from the shoulders to the hips. (Esther Carré)

However, in 227 BC the number of praetors was raised from two to four per year, one, in future, being assigned to Sardinia and one to Sicily. Ironically, the first provincial governor of Sicily was none other than Caius Flaminius, who, ten years later as a consul, was to meet his death at Trasimene.

The consuls had a wide range of functions both in peace and in war, but leadership in war was the core of the office for it was there that the consuls met their heaviest responsibilities and greatest opportunities, a chance to win *gloria* – prestige – among their fellows. Leadership in war gave the consul many powers, such as the right to appoint supplementary military tribunes, to levy and select soldiers, and to inflict both corporal and capital punishment on active service upon anyone under their command (Polybios 6.12.6–8). Serious crimes, such as the neglect of sentry duty, giving false witness, theft from comrades or sodomy, were punishable by death, with lesser misdemeanours resulting in a flogging. The death penalty was customarily administered by beating (*fustuarium*), whereupon the comrades of the condemned man mercilessly fell upon him with clubs and stones (Polybios 6.37.1–2).

In order to assist him in carrying out his duties, each consul was aided by a quaestor, who appears to have been responsible for the army's finances and rations, disposal of booty and sale of captives to the slave dealers who followed the army to carry out these transactions (Polybios 6.12.8, 31.2, cf. 14.7.3–4).

Funerary monument of Ti. Flavius Miccalus (Istanbul, Arkeoloji Müzesi, 77.7T), 1st century BC, from Perinthus (Kamara Dere). This relief depicts a legionary wielding a *gladius Hispaniensis*, the short, cut-and-thrust sword that hung from a belt on the right thigh. Note the two-edged blade and triangular point. (Esther Carré)

Centuriate

Although the legion was divided into 30 basic tactical units, the maniples, for administrative purposes were split into two centuries (*centuriae*) each commanded by a centurion (Greek *taxiarchos*, Latin *centurio*). According to Polybios each maniple had two centurions (*centuriones*) so that the unit 'should never be without a leader and commander' (6.24.6). The *centurio prior*, the first of the two to be appointed, as the title suggests, was responsible for commanding the right half of the maniple, the *centurio posterior* being in charge of the left (Polybios 6.24.7). As the maniple rather than the century (*centuria*) was the tactical unit, the *centurio prior* commanded the maniple as a whole in battle, the *centurio posterior* only taking over if the other was incapacitated. There were thus 60 *centuriones* per legion, 30 senior (*centuriones prior*) and 30 junior (*centuriones posterior*).

Centurions were either appointed by the military tribunes or, as Polybios says (6.24.1), elected from amongst the ordinary soldiers (*milites*). They were usually chosen from experienced and proven soldiers, steady rather than especially bold men, but had to be literate. Although of the same social background as the men they led, the senior centurion of the legion, known as the *centurio primi pili* (later called the *primus pilus*) and commander of the first century (and maniple) of the *triarii*, was included *ex officio* along with the military tribunes, in the consul's war-council (Polybios 6.24.2). Such men could be very experienced indeed.

There existed from at least 200 BC onwards a core of near professionals, very experienced and well-trained men who liked adventure and the risks, or who had few, if any, home ties, and who were more than glad to volunteer over a number of years. A splendid example from this period must be the career, as recorded by Livy, of the centurion Spurius Ligustinus:

I joined the army in the consulship of Publius Sulpicius and Caius Aurelius [200 BC]; and served for two years in the ranks in the army, which was taken across to Macedonia, in the campaign against King Philip [i.e. Second Macedonian War, 200–197 BC]. In the third year Quinctius Flamininus promoted me, for my bravery, centurion of the tenth maniple of *hastati*. After the defeat of Philip and the Macedonians

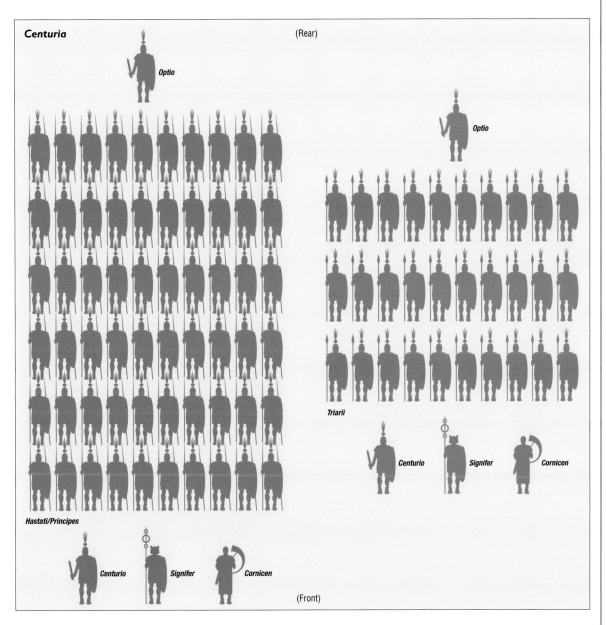

The administrative subunit in the *legio* was the century (*centuria*), two per *manipulus* (*centuria prior, centuria posterior*). These were either of 60 (*hastati, principes*) or 30 legionaries (*triarii*), each with its own centurion (*centurio*), second-in-command (*optio*), standard-bearer (*signifer*), trumpeter (*cornicen*) and guard commander (*tesserarius*). The *centurio* led by example from the front, taking a position either in the front rank itself, alongside the *signifer* and *cornicen*, or else slightly to the right of the front rank. Each *centurio* was assisted by an *optio*, a rear-rank officer who maintained unit cohesion from the rear. He took up a position either in the rear rank itself, or else behind it, which gave him a clearer view of the state of affairs in the *centuria* as a whole.

[at Kynoskephalai, 197 BC], when we had been brought back to Italy and demobilized, I immediately left for Iberia as a volunteer with the consul Marcus Porcius [195 BC]. Of all the living generals none has been a keener observer and judge of bravery than he, as is well known to those who through long military service have had experience of him and other commanders. This general judged me worthy to be appointed centurion of the first century of *hastati*. I enlisted for the third time, again as a volunteer, in the army sent against the Aetolians and King Antiochus [i.e. Syrian War, 192–189 BC]; Marcus Acilius appointed me centurion of the first century of the *principes*. When Antiochus had been driven out and the Aetolians had been crushed [at Thermopylai, 191 BC], we were brought back to Italy; and twice after that I took part in campaigns in which the legions served for a year. Thereafter I saw two campaigns in Iberia [i.e. Iberian War, 181–180 BC], one with Q. Fulvius Flaccus as praetor, the other with Ti. Sempronius Gracchus in command. Flaccus brought me back home with the others whom he brought back with him from the province for his triumph, on account of their bravery; and I returned to Iberia because I was asked to do so by Tiberius Gracchus. Four times in the course of a few years I held the rank of *centurio primi pili* [i.e. centurion of the first century of the *triarii*]; 34 times I was rewarded for bravery by the generals; I have been given six civic crowns (*coronae civicae*). I have completed 22 years of service, and I am now over 50 years old.

Livy 42.34.5–11

Ligustinus was making a plea to the consuls of 171 BC to ensure that he received an appointment appropriate to his experience and status. After his initial six years of service in Macedonia, he had re-enlisted as a volunteer, and served in Iberia, Greece, Asia and perhaps elsewhere for a further 16 years. He was showered with military decorations by a succession of admiring commanders, including M. Porcius Cato (the Censor), a general Ligustinus evidently held in high regard.

Prominent amongst his honours were the six *coronae civicae*, each an oak-leaf crown awarded for saving the life of a fellow Roman citizen in battle. Ligustinus would have worn these, as well as his other military decorations, at every public festival at home and would have commanded great respect. Such visible symbols of his valour would not be confined to the public domain, however, as it was also the Roman custom to hang up these trophies in the most conspicuous place in the house. All in all the pugnacious Ligustinus had served all but two years as a centurion, holding increasingly senior posts,

Etruscan horseman, relief decorating a cinerary urn in alabaster (Palermo, Museo Archeologico, 8462). He wears a crested Etrusco-Corinthian helmet, short cuirass with shoulder doubling and *pteruges*, and holds a large, Greek-style cavalry shield. He is armed with a sturdy spear, which possibly carries a butt-spike. (Author's collection)

culminating in that of the senior centurion (*centurio primi pili*) of the legion. As we well know, 16 years was the maximum a man could be forced to serve, but the quintagenarian Ligustinus, now with 22 years' service under his belt, went on to be *centurio primi pili* again in *legio I*, serving under the consuls in the Third Macedonian War (171–167 BC).

His pattern of service would not have been much out of place in the professional army of the Principate. Ligustinus is presented as the ideal soldier-farmer, since Livy takes care to point out that he still farmed the plot of land he had been left by his father, where his wife had borne him six sons, of whom four were grown up, and two daughters, both of whom were married. What is intriguing is that this smallholding was not of sufficient size to have rendered him liable to military service at all, and that his army service had been voluntary. The peasant family of three to four mouths needed a minimum of seven *iugera* of land to survive at subsistence level. This seven-*iugera* plot (4.55 acres/1.75ha) is very much the traditional figure for many of the *viritim* ('man-by-man') grants handed out by the state during the first half of the 2nd century BC. Ligustinus declares that his father had left him 'one *iugerum* of land and a little hut' (Livy 42.34.2). As this was less than the standard minimum of two *iugera* for landed property it is little wonder that Ligustinus had made a career out of the army.

Junior officers

Each *centurio* was assisted by a second-in-command (*optio*), the *centuriones* choosing their own *optiones* as Varro (*De Lingua Latina* 5.91) confirms, as well as a standard-bearer (*signifer*), a trumpeter (*cornicen*) and a guard commander (*tesserarius*). The *optio* traditionally stood at the rear of the *centuria* and acted as a quartermaster for his unit (Polybios 6.24.3), while the *tesserarius* supervised the posting of the sentries at night and was responsible for distributing the following day's watchword, which he received each night inscribed on a wooden tablet (*tessera*). Polybios says the *centuriones* 'choose from the ranks two of their bravest and most soldierly men to be the standard-bearers for each maniple' (6.24.5). It seems there was only one standard (*signum*) per maniple, however, so one of the standard-bearers (*signiferi*) was evidently a substitute should anything happen to the other.

Command and control in action

The Roman Army of this period functioned best at the level of the consular army, which consisted of at least 20,000 men in its entirety. It was very rare for any enemy to pose so great a threat that the two consuls were required to join forces and give battle together. On the rare occasions that this was considered necessary, as at Cannae, it was normal for the consuls to hold supreme command on alternate days (Polybios 3.110.4, 113.1).

Deeply embedded in the Roman political system, and the military hierarchy was essentially an extension of this, was the desire to prevent any one individual gaining overwhelming power. Therefore, just as in politics any grade of magistrate had several members, each with equal *imperium* who held office for one year and then returned to private life, so also in the military organization there were two *centuriones* to a *manipulus*, three *decuriones* to a *turma*, three *praefecti* to an *ala*, and six *tribuni militum* to a *legio*.

On the battlefield itself the Romans placed great emphasis on encouraging and rewarding individual boldness in soldiers of all ranks, but they also recognized the very real need for aggressive officers who would lead the men forward to fight their way through the enemy's formation. There was an *optio* behind each century to hold the men in place and a *centurio* in the front rank to urge them onwards. According to Polybios (6.24.9) a centurion was supposed to be selected for his determination and skill as a leader rather than prowess in individual fighting, and as the very nature of infantry combat drew

on this sort of characteristic, stubbornness was especially important. Unlike the centurions, however, the six military tribunes were not tied to any one position within the legion, but would move around the battle line, encouraging the men and committing reserves as necessary.

In addition to the legionary officers there was the consul, who would be close to the fighting so as to inspire his command and control the battle. Although the consular commanders did indeed get involved in the fighting, they did so prudently, and tended not to risk their own lives unless their army was clearly defeated, as was the case when L. Aemilius Paullus became actively involved in the infantry combat at Cannae (Polybios 3.116.8–9, cf. Livy 22.49.12). Instead they tended to move around behind the lines, close to the front, encouraging those in front of them and directing what reserves there were. Even so, this could still be risky. A thrown javelin was to kill P. Cornelius Scipio, the father of Scipio Africanus, when he was riding around the front lines inspiring and organizing his men (Livy 25.34.11).

Roman Army in battle

It should never be forgotten that the legions at this time were not composed of the highly disciplined, professional soldiers of later centuries, but were still a volunteer militia of citizens who looked forward to returning to civilian life as soon as a campaign was over and the threat to their state ended. The campaign season opened in March and closed in October, as official festivals in the Roman calendar make clear.

Roman strength lay in the set-piece battle, the decisive clash of opposing armies that settled the issue one way or another. Polybios (1.37.7–10) saw the

Bronze *kopis* and iron *falcata* (Paris, musée de l'armée, J 1234, B 38). The *falcata* (right), a short but deadly sword employed by the Iberians, was a direct copy of the Greek *kopis* (left). Like the *kopis*, the *falcata* had a single-edged blade that widened towards the point, thereby increasing the kinetic energy of a blow. (Esther Carré)

Romans as rather oldfashioned in their straightforward and open approach to warfare, commenting that as a race they tended to rely instinctively on 'brute force' (*bía*) when making war. Nothing illustrates his criticism better than Cannae, when Roman tactics subordinated the other arms very much to the heavy infantry.

Roman tactical doctrine and practice

The essential philosophy behind the manipular legion was that of winning a straightforward, mass engagement with the enemy. Only in the method of doing this did it differ from the Greek phalanx or Macedonian combination of this with shock cavalry (e.g. Second Koroneia 394 BC, Gaugamela 331 BC). The same, quick decisive clash with the enemy was desired. In this role the manipular legion performed very well. Hannibal's obvious skill as a general inflicted a number of massive defeats on this army (e.g. Cannae 216 BC), yet the same type of army, when better led and with higher morale, beat him in turn (i.e. Zama 202 BC). As Polybios rightly says, 'the defeats they suffered had nothing to do with weapons or formations, but were brought about by Hannibal's cleverness and military genius' (18.28.7).

The inclusion of allied troops within the armies of this period did not change the essential tactical doctrines behind them. Many allied units were organized and equipped as legions and thus acted in a similar fashion, whilst the additional light-armed troops or cavalry were deployed to help achieve the same aim of breaking the enemy line.

Legion

Polybios does not offer his readers an account of the legion in battle, but there are a number of combat descriptions both in his own work and that of Livy. However, very few accounts describe tactics in detail; a contemporary Roman (or Greek) audience would take much for granted.

Even so, the legion would usually approach the enemy in its standard battle formation, the *triplex acies*, which was based around the triple line of *hastati*, *principes* and *triarii*, with the *velites* forming a light screen in front. Each of the three lines consisted of ten maniples. The maniples were not drawn up side by side, but gaps were left equal in width to their own frontage (*c.*18m). The gaps in the line of the *hastati* were covered in the second line by the maniples of the more seasoned *principes*, and likewise the maniples of the veteran *triarii* covered the gaps in the line of the *principes*. Modern commentators conveniently call this battle formation the *quincunx*, from the five dots on a dice-cube.

Battle would be opened by the *velites* who attempted to disorganize and unsettle enemy formations with a hail of javelins. This done, they retired through the gaps in the maniples of the *hastati* and made their way to the rear. The maniples of the *hastati* now reformed to close the gaps, either by each maniple extending its frontage, thus giving individuals more room in which to handle their weapons, or, if the maniple was drawn up two centuries deep, the *centurio posterior* would move his *centuria* to the left and forward, thus running out and forming up alongside the *centuria* of the *centurio prior* in the line itself (Keppie 1998: 38–39).

The *hastati* would discharge their *pila*, throwing first their light and then their heavyweight *pila*, some 15m – the effective range of a *pilum* – from the enemy. The term *hastati*, spearmen, should be taken to mean armed with throwing spears, namely *pila*, instead of thrusting ones. This is after all the sense it bears out in our earliest surviving example of it, in Ennius' line *hastati spargunt hasti*, 'hastati who hurl *hasti*' (fr. 284 Vahlen)[8], and their name probably reflects a time when they alone used *pila*. If the *pila* did not actually

---

8 Not long after the Second Punic War, Quintus Ennius (239–169 BC) wrote an epic poem entitled *Annales* on the history of Rome from its origins, fragments of which survive. Born in Rudiae, Calabria, he had served in the Roman Army, presumably in an allied *ala*.

hit the enemy, they would often become embedded in their shields, their barbed points making them difficult to withdraw. Handicapped by a *pilum* the shield became useless. Additionally, the thin metal shaft bent or buckled on impact thus preventing the weapon being thrown back.

During the confusion caused by this hail of *pila*, which could be devastating, the *hastati* drew their swords and, says Polybios, 'charged the enemy yelling

Vachères warrior (Vachères, musée municipal), 1st century BC, shows the characteristic iron mail-shirt, heavy cloak, tubular torc and sword-belt of the aristocratic Celtic warrior. A long slashing-sword, for all to see, hangs at his right hip and he leans on his shield in characteristic Gallic fashion. (Author's collection)

Manipular tactics

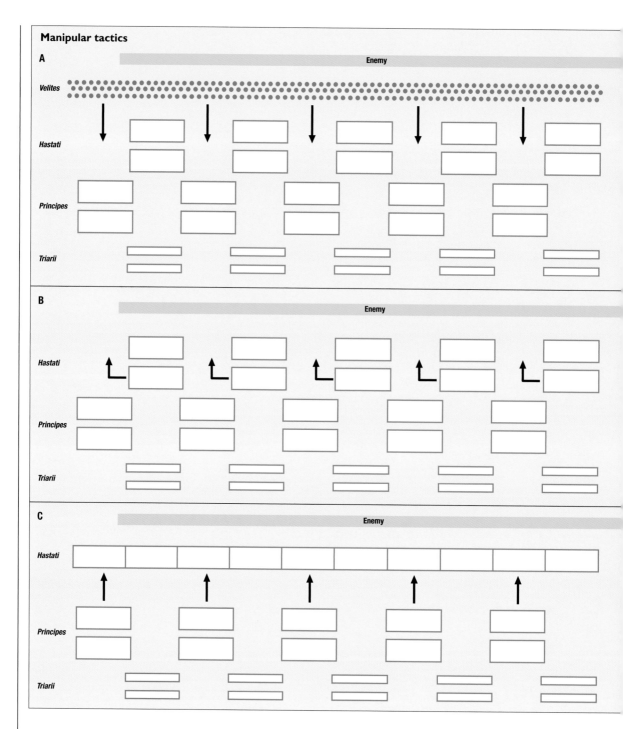

The manipular system allows the reinforcement of the fighting line with fresh troops, with the intention that their enthusiasm would persuade the whole line to surge forward into contact once again against the fatigued enemy. The reserve lines can reinforce the fighting line if it is coming under pressure, or advance to exploit any successes and breakthroughs it has managed to achieve. The *tribuni militum*, who have pressed forward to oversee the fighting, are not there just to inspire the men and witness their behaviour, but also to control the commitment of the second and third lines.

Phase A

The *legio* is drawn up in three lines, initially with its *manipuli* drawn up two *centuriae* deep, the *centuria posterior* behind the *centuria prior*. The battle is begun by the *velites*, who attempt to harass the enemy as it advances with missile fire. On a given signal, the *velites* retire through the gaps.

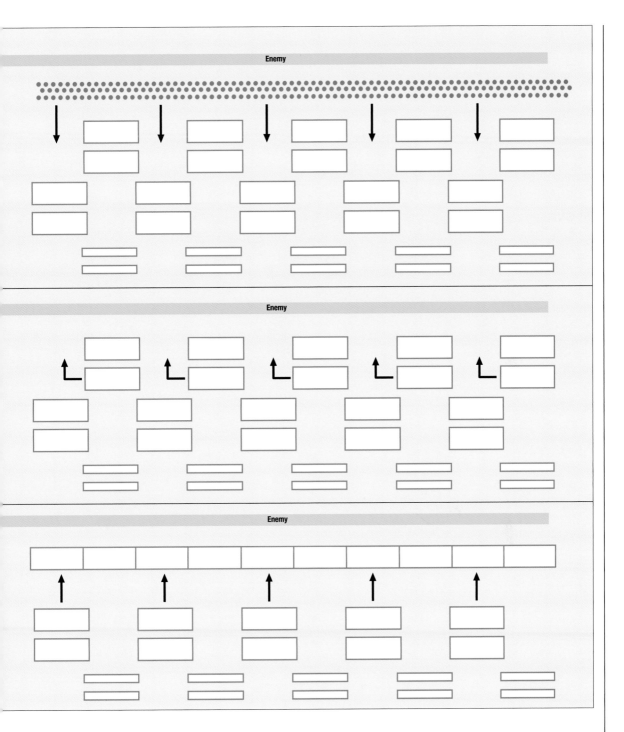

Phase B

The *velites* through, the *hastati* close the gaps in their line, the *centuria posterior* moving alongside the *centuria prior*. Having dressed their ranks, the *hastati* hurl their *pila*, draw their swords and charge into contact. They now constitute the fighting line of the *legio*.

Phase C

The initial charge has failed to break the enemy, and the momentum of the attack has been dissipated. The *hastati* are now hard pressed, so the *principes* are ordered up to reinforce the fighting line.

Frieze decorating victory (Pydna 168 BC) monument of Aemilius Paullus (Delphi, Archaeological Museum), son of the L. Aemilius Paullus killed at Cannae. From left to right, a legionary fighting a Macedonian cavalryman, a legionary in a mail shirt, and a Latin/Italian cavalryman also in a mail shirt. (Author's collection)

their war cry and clashing their weapons against their shields as is their custom' (15.12.8, cf. 1.34.2). He also says (18.30.6–8) the Romans formed up in a much looser formation than other heavy infantry, adding this was necessary to use the sword and for the soldier to defend himself all round with his shield. This implies the legionary was essentially an individual fighter, a swordsman. Yet M. Porcius Cato (the Censor), who served during the Second Punic War as an *eques* and quaestor, always maintained that a soldier's bearing, confidence and the ferociousness of his war cry were more important than his actual skill with a blade (Plutarch *Cato the Censor* 1).

In his brief description of the *gladius Hispaniensis* (Greek *Iberikós*) Polybios evidently says it was 'worn high on the right thigh' so as to be clear of the legs, adding that it was an excellent weapon 'for thrusting, and both of its edges cut effectually, as the blade is very strong and firm' (6.23.6–7). The wearing of the sword on the right side goes back to the Iberians, and before them, to the Celts. The sword was the weapon of the high-status warrior, and to carry one was to display a symbol of rank and prestige. It was probably for cultural reasons alone, therefore, that the Celts carried the long slashing-sword on the right side. Usually a sword was worn on the left, the side covered by the shield, which meant the weapon was hidden from view.

If, at this early date, the legionary already carried his sword on the right-hand side suspended by a sword (waist) belt, it would not be for any cultural reason. As opposed to a scabbard-slide, the four-ring suspension system on his scabbard enabled the legionary to draw his weapon quickly with the right hand, an asset in close-quarter combat. In view of its relatively short blade, inverting the hand to grasp the hilt and pushing the pommel forward drew the *gladius* with ease. With its sharp point and four-ring suspension arrangement, the Delos sword, firmly dated to 69 BC, shows all the characteristics of the *gladius* described a century earlier by Polybios. Another such example is the Mouriès sword, found in a tomb in association with a group of pottery and metal artefacts, notably a bronze washing-kit with an Italic jug and *patera*. This assembly can be dated to around the turn of the 1st century BC (Bishop and Coulston 1993: 53, Feugère 2002: 79).

Polybios, in an excursion dedicated to the comparison between Roman and Macedonian military equipment and tactical formations, says the following:

> According to the Roman methods of fighting each man makes his movements individually: not only does he defend his body with his long shield, constantly moving it to meet a threatened blow, but he uses his sword both for cutting and for thrusting.
> Polybios 18.30.6

What we are witnessing here is the intelligent use, by a swordsman, of the short sword. It appears, therefore, that the tactical doctrine commonly associated with the imperial Roman legion was already in place during Polybios' day.

Left-hand side of cinerary urn in alabaster (Volterra, Museo Etrusco, MG 278), 2nd century BC. The relief depicts an Etruscan horseman wearing a short mail shirt with shoulder doubling and *pteruges*. He also wears an Etrusco-Corinthian helmet. The staff most likely denotes rank, conceivably that of *decurio*. (Author's collection)

We know from the archaeological record that the *gladius* of the Principate ('Pompeii' type) was an amazingly light and well-balanced weapon that was capable of making blindingly fast attacks, and was suitable for both cuts and thrusts. However, Tacitus (b. *c.* AD 56) and Vegetius (*fl. c.* AD 385) lay great stress on the *gladius* being employed by the legionary for thrusting rather than slashing. As Vegetius rightly says, 'a slash-cut, whatever its force, seldom kills' (1.12), and thus a thrust was certainly more likely to deliver the fatal wound. Having thrown the *pilum* and charged into contact, the standard drill for the imperial legionary was to punch the enemy in the face with the shield-boss and then jab him in the belly with the razor-sharp point of the sword (Tacitus *Annales* 2.14, 21, 14.36, *Historiae* 2.42, *Agricola* 36.2).

In his near-contemporary account of the battle of Telamon (225 BC), Polybios tells us that 'Roman shields … were far better designed for defence, and so were their swords for attack, since the Gallic sword can only be used for cutting and not for thrusting' (2.30.9). Soon after, when he covers the Gallic *tumultus* of 223 BC, it is disclosed that legionaries 'made no attempt to slash and used only the thrust, kept their swords straight and relied on their sharp points … inflicting one wound after another on the breast or the face' (2.33.6). In a much later passage (6.23.4) he hints that they were trained to take the first whirling blow of the Celtic slashing-sword on the rim of the *scutum*, which was suitably bound with iron.

The use of the thrust also meant the legionary kept most of his torso well covered, and thus protected, by his *scutum*. The latter, having absorbed the attack of his antagonist, was now punched into the face of the opponent as the legionary stepped forward to jab with his *gladius*. Much like the riot shield of a

Reconstruction Gallic arms and armour, archaeological open day, Bobigny, Seine-Saint-Denis. Here we see the characteristic long slashing-sword of the Gallic warrior. It was certainly not contrived for finesse, but a weapon designed to either hack an opponent to pieces or to beat him to a bloody pulp. (Esther Carré)

modern policeman, the *scutum* was used both defensively and offensively to defect blows and hammer into the opponent's shield or body to create openings. As he stood with his left foot forward, a legionary could get much of his bodyweight behind this punch. Added to this was the considerable weight of the *scutum* itself.

Ideally, the *hastati* fought the main enemy line to a standstill, but if they were rebuffed, or lost momentum, the *principes* advanced into the combat zone and the process was repeated. Hand-to-hand fighting was physically strenuous and emotionally draining, and the skill of a Roman commander lay in committing his second and third lines at the right time. Obviously the survivors of the *hastati* and the *principes* now reinforced the *triarii* if it came down to a final trial of strength. The phrase *inde rem ad triarios redisse*, 'the last resource is in the *triarii*' (Livy 8.8.9) passed into the Latin tongue as a description of a desperate situation.

Victory would eventually go to the side that endured the stress of staying so close to the enemy for the longest and was still able to urge enough of its men forward to renew the fighting. It was the inherent flexibility of the manipular system that made the legion a formidable battlefield opponent. In Polybios' measured analysis:

> The order of battle used by the Roman army is very difficult to break through, since it allows every man to fight both individually and collectively; the effect is to offer a formation that can present a front in any direction, since the maniples that are nearest to the point where danger threatens wheel in order to meet it. The arms they carry both give protection and also instil great confidence into the men, because of the size of the shields and the strength of the swords, which can withstand repeated blows. All these factors make the Romans formidable antagonists in battle and very hard to overcome.
> Polybios 15.15.7–10

Hellenistic armies, for instance, preferred to deepen their phalanx rather than form troops into a second line, and made little use of reserves, as the commander's role was usually to charge at the head of his cavalry in the manner of Alexander the Great. The deepening of the pike-armed phalanx gave it so much stamina in the mêlée, but even the men in the rear ranks were affected by the stress and exhaustion of prolonged combat. The Roman system, on the other hand, allowed fresh men to be fed into the fighting line, renewing its impetus and leading a surge forward, which might well have been enough to break a wearying enemy.

Socii

In a consular army, the two Roman legions would form the centre with two allied *alae* deployed on their flanks – they were known as the '*ala* of the left' and the '*ala* of the right' (Polybios 6.26.9), a positioning reflecting the term *ala*, wing. In larger armies, however, *legiones* and *alae* would probably alternate as they did at Cannae, where there were effectively four separate consular armies, each consisting of two *legiones* and two *alae*, and each with its own commander. Although the *extraordinarii* had a special place in the line-of-march (*agmen*) and in camp (Polybios 6.31.2, 6, 8, 40.4, 8), they do not seem to have had a special role in battle and may have simply stood with the rest of the allies, that is, as part of their parent unit.

Polybios' silence on the subject suggests that the allies were organized and equipped along Roman lines, which would certainly have been desirable as it would have enabled them to interact smoothly with the legions. Presumably their traditional arms and tactics were gradually replaced by Roman methods and weaponry (Lazenby 1978: 13).

Dying Gaul (Rome, Musei Capitolini, MC 747), Roman copy of the 2nd-century Pergamene original. Initially the Romans were terrified by these bigger-than-life warriors, who adorned themselves with torques, wore long moustaches and had hair that was slaked with lime to make it stand up like a horse's mane. (Author's collection)

Light troops

Roman *velites* were essentially skirmishers, who would open a battle screening the heavy infantry, withdraw through their ranks, regroup on the *triarii* and either stay in reserve or threaten the enemy's flanks. Skirmishers operated in a very loose order, with wide gaps between men to ensure that they could easily move to avoid incoming missiles. The loose and fluid formation thus employed allowed each man great freedom to advance and retire at will.

In ideal circumstances skirmishers were supposed to drive back their opposite numbers and then begin to 'soften up' the main body of the enemy, but such successes were exceptionally rare. *Velites* appear not to have had their own officers, being commanded by the centurions stationed with the heavy infantry, yet they could be quite effective in battle. Probably relying on 'natural leaders' for tactical command, Livy (31.35.4–6, 38.21.12–13) describes them successfully skirmishing from a distance by throwing their javelins and then fighting at close quarters with their swords, using their shields to protect themselves. Polybios (6.22.3) mentions how certain *velites* would wear a wolf's skin over their helmets so that they would be visible to their centurions from a distance; such individuals, being keen to impress, could well have led by example.

A high degree of courage would have been required in order to get close enough to hit the enemy, necessitating the need to enter the killing zone and exposing oneself as an individual to enemy fire. Thus the main importance of preliminary skirmishing was probably morale or psychological. Ancient writers are certainly right to regard this initial phase of battle as inconclusive and tactically insignificant, since it is quite likely that comparably few troops were killed or even wounded in it.

Lightly armed troops could also support cavalry. Outside Capua (211 BC), to compensate for the superiority in cavalry of the Campani, a picked body of *velites* rode pillion behind Roman cavalry, dismounted when close to the enemy horse and hurled their javelins. The surprised Campani were then charged by the cavalry and broken (Livy 26.4.5–8).

Cavalry

Cavalry served basically to protect the flanks of the consular army. The citizen-cavalry of the two legions are usually depicted as stationed on the right wing, the position of honour, whilst the Latin and Italian cavalry formed on the left. Still, given that there were often three times as many of the latter as the former, this may be an oversimplification. Even so, combat between cavalry invariably took place on the edges of the battlefield, flanking the general infantry contest.

Terracotta figurine of Gallic warrior (Oxford, Ashmolean Museum). Gauls normally fought stripped to the waist in just trousers, usually plaid and tied at the ankles, though they might retain the *sagum*, the traditional Celtic cloak. Under a first-class general such as Hannibal, Gauls made excellent soldiers. (Author's collection)

Under normal circumstances, one side would apparently have been intimidated by the other and given way before colliding with them. This seems reasonable, for horses will not charge into solid objects, and a steady unit of enemy horsemen in close formation could well have been perceived as just an impenetrable object. Moreover, the riders would themselves have been all too aware of the potential catastrophe that could occur if the opposing forces crashed into each other. Under normal circumstances the riders' nerve would fail. Steady cavalry nearly always relied upon morale rather than physical shock to cause the enemy to flinch, break and run.

Engineering

Despite being a militia force, the engineering feats of the middle-republican army symbolized the ordered existence of citizens whilst they served in the legions. Pyrrhos of Epeiros is supposed to have realized that he was not dealing with mere barbarians when he saw the order of the Roman camp (Plutarch *Pyrrhos* 16.5). Oddly enough, Frontinus (*Strategemata* 4.1.14, cf. Livy 35.14.6) claims that the Romans developed the idea of a marching camp after defeating Pyrrhos on the Arusian Plains near Maleventum (275 BC), capturing his camp and noting its design. Whatever, by Polybios' day constructing a formally laid-out camp protected by a rampart and a ditch was a routine procedure.

Marching camps

In accordance with the invariable Roman custom of a rigid daily routine, the legionaries constructed an entrenchment to fortify their camp every night after the day's march. Polybios spells out the drills by which these marching camps were erected.

The via Appia built in 312 BC on the initiative of the censor Ap. Claudius Caecus. This road made it easy for Roman troops to move between Rome and the new conquest of Capua. Initially 211km long, this road was later extended to Brundisium via Tarentum. (Author's collection)

As the consular army neared the end of the march one of the military tribunes and the centurions who formed the camp surveying team were sent ahead to select a site for the camp. The site had to be open, preferably on rising ground and with no cover that could be exploited by the enemy. The camp itself covered an area about four *plethra* (700m²). A point which afforded maximum visibility was selected for the site of the consul's tent (*praetorium*) and a white flag was placed on the spot. A red flag was set up on the side nearest water. Here the *legiones* and *alae* would camp (Polybios 6.27.1–4).

A ditch, some three Roman feet (0.9m) deep and four feet (1.2m) wide, normally surrounded a marching camp. The spoil was piled up on the inside, faced with turf and levelled off to form a low rampart (*agger*). The two legions constructed the defences at the front and rear of the camp, while the right and left *alae* of the allies built the right and left sides respectively. Each maniple was allotted a section about 25m long. The centurions checked that the work of their maniples was done properly, while a pair of military tribunes or prefects supervised the overall effort on each side of the camp (Polybios 6.34.1–3).

Far stronger defences were needed when camping close to the enemy and the work was likely to be hampered by attacks. Therefore as the army arrived, all the cavalry, the light-armed troops and half of the heavy infantry were deployed in battle array in front of the projected line of the ditch facing the enemy. The baggage train was placed behind the line of the rampart and the remainder of the troops began to dig in. They dug a ditch nine Roman feet (2.7m) deep and 12 feet (3.6m) wide, piling up the spoil on the inside to form a turf-faced rampart four feet (1.2m) high. On the march each soldier carried a bundle of sharpened stakes, usually cut from sturdy branches. These were planted close together in the top of the rampart to form a palisade (*vallum*). As work proceeded, the heavy infantry were gradually withdrawn from the battle line, maniple by maniple, starting with the *triarii* who were nearest the rampart. These troops were put to work digging the other sides of the camp. The cavalry were not withdrawn until the defences facing the enemy were complete.

These defences offered protection against surprise attack, the ditch and rampart being sufficient only to delay attackers and not to stop them. The Romans rarely, if ever, planned to fight from within the camp, but to advance and meet the enemy in the field. Between the rampart-line and the tent-lines of a camp, a distance of 200 Roman feet (60m), was an open area known as the *intervallum*, which ensured that the tents were out of range of missiles thrown or shot from beyond the defences. More importantly, this space allowed the army to form itself up ready to deploy into battle order.

The marching camp was a highly organized, neatly laid-out structure with the legions divided into lines and maniples. Always built to recognizably the same pattern, a camp had four gateways (*portae praetoria, principalis dextra, decumana* and *principalis sinistra*) and two main roads (*viae principalis* and *praetoria*) running at 90 degrees and meeting in front of the main concentration of command tents (*praetorium* and *quaestorium*). Everything was regulated, from the positioning of each unit's tents and baggage to the duties carried out by various contingents, so that for instance the *triarii* always provided guards for the horse-lines. The responsibilities of various officers to supervise the sentries and pickets around the camp and to transmit orders for the next day's march were all clearly allocated.

Roads

As with most Mediterranean lands, Italy is fairly divided into mountains and plains. However, it differs from Greece in that the plains are more continuous. For much of the peninsula, especially on the east coast, it is possible to follow coastal plains (Latium, Campanian), albeit narrow in some cases, for considerable distances, but then great massifs that run down steeply to the sea interrupt passage. Travellers, therefore, have to negotiate difficult narrow mountain paths to get from one coastal plain to another. Communication across the mountains was even more difficult (Alps, Apennines). The larger Apennine rivers (Liras, Volturno) are tortuous, and lead to high watersheds, so that crossing the mountains from east to west was very difficult. The topography of Italy, therefore, encourages regional separatism, and it was thus rational of the Romans to build a series of great roads across the mountains to facilitate the movement of troops and unify the peninsula.

It was the Romans who created (or at least who made possible) the concept of Italy, as we understand today. Roman roads provided direct, well-maintained routes along which an army could move with ease. An important aspect of Rome's absorption of conquered territory was to construct roads linking new colonies to Rome. In Italy itself, the roads tended to follow Rome's conquests both in time and space. With the annexation of Veii (396 BC), the Etruscan city that had been Rome's chief rival for supremacy in the Tiber plain, we see its citizen-army move against the rest of Latium and then up into the Apennine fastness of the Samnites. Next came the turn of Etruria and Umbria to the north (viae Aurelia, Flaminia and Aemilia), with Campania to the south soon to follow, then Lucania and the Greek *poleis* of southern Italy (via Appia). Built on a monumental scale, these roads combined practical utility with visually impressive statements of power.

There was nothing revolutionary in the principles behind Roman roads. They were laid with care, on gravel foundations that allowed the soil beneath the surface to drain, and they were often paved on top with stone flags. Ditches along the sides improved drainage, and roads had a tendency to follow the ridges of river valleys, which had the additional effect of helping to prevent erosion on the slopes. The Greeks knew most of these principles, and the Romans picked others up from the Etruscans, who were no mean road-builders themselves.

The milestone was another device that the Romans did not invent, but which they applied more methodically than anyone had done before. As a reflection of the military purpose of the roads, the stones marked 1,000 (*mille*) paces of a Roman legionary. The Romans measured a double pace, that is, the interval between the first foot leaving the ground to when the second touches it again.

Siegecraft

The ability to reduce strongholds by siege was as important as victory in pitched battle. During this period the Romans were involved in many sieges varying from minor hill forts to major cities, notably Agrigentum (262–261 BC), Syracuse (213–212 BC), Capua (212–211 BC), New Carthage (209 BC), Carthage (149–146 BC) and Numantia (134–133 BC). Interestingly, Polybios probably witnessed the last two in the company of his chief patron, P. Cornelius Scipio Aemilianus, grandson of the L. Aemilius Paullus killed at Cannae and grandson by adoption of Scipio Africanus.

Assault was the one aspect of ancient warfare most affected by technological advances. It involved the attacker finding a way over, through or under the defender's fortifications. The simplest method was escalade, when the attacking troops carried ladders up to the walls and attempted to scale them, but this sort of operation invariably involved heavy casualties and was rarely successful unless the walls were denuded of defenders. The hazards of such an enterprise are well illustrated by Polybios' description (10.13.5–10) of the Roman assault against the walls of New Carthage (spring 209 BC). It should be noted that mobile siege towers that dropped a drawbridge onto a rampart and allowed men to cross, whilst providing covering fire from archers or artillery on top, were essentially an extension of this same basic idea.

The main alternative was to create a breach in the walls by battering ram or tunnelling underneath to undermine them. This required extensive preparation, technical knowledge and labour to create siege works allowing engines such as a battering ram to pass over any defensive ditches and reach the wall. All the time the defender would be employing artillery to hinder this activity, counter-mining to thwart the attacker's tunnelling, and launching sallies to burn his engines. Sieges tended to consist of move and counter-move as the attacker and defender employed their engineering skill and massive labour to gain an advantage or negate a project begun by the other side. Yet once the defences had been breached or undermined, then this ingenuity and scientific skill counted for little as the assaulting troops had to storm their way inside. Casualties might still be heavy, and failure was a real possibility. Such was the massive effort and the uncertainty of the outcome that assaults on major cities were not contemplated lightly.

Convention decreed that a defender would normally only be permitted to surrender on terms if he did so before the first battering ram touched the wall, otherwise the city would be subject to a sack and its surviving inhabitants sold into slavery. Having seized Agrigentum (261 BC), for instance, the Romans comprehensively sacked the city, selling its Greek inhabitants – 25,000 according to Diodoros (23.9.1) – into slavery (Polybios 1.19.14–15). Polybios tells us that he had witnessed the aftermath of the Roman sack of a city – probably when he had accompanied Scipio Aemilianus on campaign in Africa or Iberia – and had seen the dismembered bodies of men and even animals lying in the streets. Polybios (10.15.5–6) believed that such atrocities were intended to inspire terror, both to overawe the population and prevent further resistance, but also to deter other cities from opposing a Roman army. The Roman sack of a city was brutal even by the standards of the day, which assumed general massacre of men and rape of women.

At this period the Roman Army, unlike the professional Hellenistic armies, lacked the technical skill to undertake such a project on a major city with any real prospect of success. The seaward assault on Syracuse (spring 213 BC), under the personal command of M. Claudius Marcellus, is a good illustration of this. Marcellus had removed the oar ports from four quinqueremes, and the starboard oars from four more, then lashed them together two by two. On the bows were erected huge scaling-ladders, protected by wickerwork screens, top and sides, which could be lowered by pulleys attached to the masts – the complete contraptions were known as *sambucae*, harps, from their shape.

West wall of Castello Eurialo, Syracuse, with its distinctive silhouette of five ruined towers. Siege warfare was not a speciality of the Romans, unlike the Greeks, and Marcellus rejected the idea of a full-scale attack on the five-tower complex (212 BC), recently upgraded by Archimedes, without hesitation. (Author's collection)

A Roman sack was brutal even by the standards of the day. Having captured and sacked Agrigentum (261 BC), they sold the survivors, 25,000 it is said, into slavery. South walls of the *polis*, seen here looking from the temple of Hera to that of Concordia. (Author's collection)

But the Romans had reckoned without the ingenuity of the defenders, inspired by the genius-scientist, Archimedes. He had not only constructed a series of catapults designed to throw stones and bolts at various ranges, which caused severe casualties as the Roman ships approached, but he had also prepared wooden arms on pivots that swung over the walls to drop large rocks and lumps of lead onto the *sambucae*, or let down an 'iron hand' at the end of a chain that seized the prows of the ships, lifted them into the air by means of a counterweight, and then let them fall with disastrous effect (Polybios 8.4–6.6). Later tradition even credited him with concentrating the sun's rays by means of giant lenses to set fire to the Roman ships (Diodoros 26.18, Zonaras 9.4). Similar devices also helped to beat off the landward attack, led by Marcellus' lieutenant the propraetor Ap. Claudius Pulcher, with heavy losses (Polybios 8.7.1–6). The Romans were thus forced to abandon the idea of taking the city by assault.

This meant that the only viable option available was blockade, cutting off the city from the outside world until its food supplies ran out and starvation forced surrender. If an enemy had had time to prepare for the siege by massing stocks of essentials, then this might well take a very long time. With a large enough force the attacker would throw up a system of ditches and small forts that completely surrounded the city so as to blockade it effectively. This project would not only consist of a line of circumvallation, but also a second line facing outwards, or a line of contravallation, built to prevent supply columns or relief forces from trying to break in. Blockade was the most common and successful means of taking a city, but it was still a difficult task, requiring a sizeable force to remain in one area for a considerable period of time. Nor was success guaranteed.

Second Punic War

Campanian plate (Rome, Museo Nazionale di Villa Giulia) showing a war elephant and calf. Unmistakably an Indian elephant (*Elephas indicus*), and possibly one of those brought by Pyrrhos of Epeiros. Nearly 3m high at the shoulders, this breed is large enough to carry a howdah. (Author's collection)

At the end of the First Punic War Carthage had lost Sicily, seapower and security. It was in this weakened condition that the once proud Carthage would witness the unprincipled seizure by Rome of Sardinia and then be forced to pay an added indemnity of 1,200 Euboian talents. It can be argued, therefore, that Hannibal (and Carthage) provoked the second war to reverse the decision of the first and its sordid aftermath and, by permanently weakening Rome, to make Carthage's western Mediterranean empire safe. Hamilcar Barca and his successors in Iberia, building on the footholds Carthage already had in the peninsula, created an empire based on the valley of the river Baetis (Guadalquivir) and the fertile territory of the Contestani in what is now Murcia (Polybios 2.1.5–9, 13.1–7, 36.3, 3.10.5–6, 39.3–4). Iberia gave the Barcids and, depending on the view taken of the independence of their power, Carthage a formidable military force and the wealth to support it.

Hannibal Barca (247–183 BC)

The Carthaginians certainly have, in our eyes at least, the romantic glamour of the doomed. The Romans destroyed their city and culture at a time when middle-republican Rome was the aggressive bully of the Mediterranean. Yet nothing is inevitable in history, and the Carthaginians put up far more resistance than any of the Hellenistic kingdoms, and came close, during the second in a series of three struggles, to destroying Roman power completely.

Their commander-in-chief during this titanic struggle was Hannibal, the eldest son of the charismatic general Hamilcar Barca (d. 229 BC), and one of the greatest generals of antiquity. Although Hannibal rated himself as third after Alexander the Great and Pyrrhos of Epeiros (Livy 35.14.5–8, cf. Plutarch *Flamininus* 21.3), he was overly modest. His victories were certainly more impressive than those of Pyrrhos were, and his strategic focus was clearer. Although Alexander achieved spectacular conquests, he did so using the superb Macedonian Army created by his father, Philip II of Macedon, whereas Hannibal achieved his continuous run of successes with an ad-hoc collection of polyglot mercenaries.

Hannibal, who was born shortly before or after his father's departure for Sicily (247 BC), probably never saw him until he returned to Carthage after the First Punic War was over. Nevertheless, the absentee parent apparently ensured his son had a good education that included a strong Greek element. Later on Hannibal was to take Greek historians with him on his expedition, including the Spartan Sosylos, his former tutor who had taught him Greek (Nepos *Hannibal* 13.3, cf. Cicero *De Oratore* 2.18.75). He then spent his youth in Iberia learning the trades of war and politics by his father's side (Zonaras 8.21) and serving under Hasdrubal the Splendid, his brother-in-law, as his second-in-command-cum-cavalry-commander (Livy 21.4.3–5, 8, Appian *Iberica* 6, Nepos *Hannibal* 3.1).

In Sicily Hamilcar had successfully maintained a struggle against the Roman forces in the north-western corner of the island until the Punic defeat at sea left him no alternative but to open negotiations, the Carthaginian government having given him full powers to handle the situation. During this twilight period of the conflict, Hamilcar, whom Polybios considered the ablest commander on either side 'both in daring and in genius' (1.64.6), displayed his talent

in low-level raiding, skirmishing and ambushing. He had the art, which he transmitted to Hannibal, of binding to himself the mercenary armies of the state by a close personal tie that was proof against all temptation.

It is of little surprise, therefore, that Hannibal had learnt his professionalism and confidence as a fighting soldier from his father, and there is more than a hint of Hamilcar, albeit on a grander scale, in his son's ability to maintain himself and his army in a foreign land for so many years. It is possible that he also inherited the plan for attacking Italy, for his father had once raided the southern Italian coast 'devastating the territory of Locri and the Bruttii' (Polybios 1.56.3). Ironically, it was his father who was the first to style himself Barca (*Bârâq*), the Semitic word for lightning-flash, and his brilliant progeny was to certainly honour the family moniker. The poet Florus (1.22) compared Hannibal and his army to a thunderbolt, which had burst its way through the middle of the Alps and descended upon Italy as if launched from the skies. If Hannibal had learned his battle tactics from his father, as a strategist he was in a class all his own.

His strategy has been criticized for failing to comprehend the nature of the Roman-led confederation and to ensure that adequate reinforcements came either by sea from Africa or land from Iberia. Yet Hannibal himself could not be everywhere, and there is no doubt that this was the only way that Carthage could ever have defeated Rome. The audacity of the march to Italy remains breathtaking, and we should not underestimate how near it came to success. His genius as a battlefield commander has seldom been questioned. It rested on a mixture of bluff and double bluff, and ability to use all types of troops to their best advantage. Cannae remains an ideal to which generations of subsequent generals have aspired, but perhaps the clearest light on Hannibal's character is shown by the fact that although he maintained his polyglot army permanently on active service in enemy territory for 15 unbroken years, he kept it 'free from sedition towards him or among themselves ... the ability of their commander forced men so radically different to give ear to a single word of command and yield obedience to a single will' (Polybios 11.19.3, 5). If this is how Polybios saw Hannibal, then his inspirational leadership and canny man-management must have been unsurpassed.

Hannibal's revenge

When Polybios (3.9.6) came to analyze the causes of the second war between Rome and Carthage, he may have been right to put first what he calls the 'wrath' (*thymós*) of Hamilcar, his anger at the end of the first war when he was forced to surrender despite remaining undefeated in Sicily. Polybios later justifies his view that Hamilcar's bitter attitude contributed towards the outbreak of a war, which only began ten years after his death, by telling the famous story of Hannibal's oath. The oath, sworn at the temple of Ba'al Shamim to his father before their departure to Iberia in 237 BC, was 'never to show goodwill to the Romans' (3.11.7).

The story has inevitably been doubted, but Polybios says that Hannibal himself told it to Antiochos III when he was later serving the king, who was bogged down in a war with Rome, as a military advisor. The view that the Second Punic War was thus a war of revenge certainly gained widespread credence among the Romans (Livy 21.1.4–5, Nepos *Hannibal* 1.2–6). It is, perhaps, most dramatically expressed by Virgil (*Aeneid* 4.622–27) when he has the Carthaginian queen Dido, heartbroken and furious at her desertion by Aeneas, curse him and his whole race and calls upon 'an avenger who shall pursue these fugitives from Troy with fire and sword'. She then fell on Aeneas' sword and killed herself. With such artistry did Virgil introduce Hannibal into his epic without naming him. Whatever, it would seem that all the leading officers swore the oath, not just Hannibal, and the oath they swore was not vengeance on Rome but a promise never to be 'a friend of Rome'. This is important phraseology: in those days the term 'a friend of Rome' implied a vassal state of Rome, such as Hieron II of Syracuse.

It is true that neither Hamilcar himself, nor his immediate successor in Iberia, his son-in-law Hasdrubal the Splendid (d. 221 BC), made any overt move

Hannibal in Italy, fresco (1503–08) attributed to the Bolognese painter, Jacopo Ripandi, in the Palazzo dei Conservatori, Rome. Looking very oriental, Hannibal rides an elephant. It is said that when he crossed the great morass that was the Arno Valley, the general himself rode his last surviving elephant. (Esther Carré)

against Rome, but we do not know how much they influenced the young Hannibal, and it is his attitude that is important.[9] Telling is his forthright attack upon Saguntum (November 219 BC), a town that he knew to be under Rome's protection, less than two years after he succeeded to the command of the Punic forces in Iberia (Polybios 3.30.1, cf. Livy 21.2.7).

Situated on a hill a little over 1km from the sea, Saguntum (Sagunto) was an Iberian town halfway between New Carthage (Cartagena) and the river Iber (Ebro). Certainly before 220 BC Hannibal had left the town untouched so as not to provoke the Romans before he was ready (Polybios 3.14.10). Telling also is the bold and decisive way in which he matured his plans for the invasion of Italy in 218 BC. Together, it at least suggests Hannibal was not too unwilling to have war with Rome. Alternatively, we can easily accuse the Romans of double-dealing as Saguntum lies far south of the Iber. If the terms of the Iber Treaty prevented them from crossing the river under arms, as it did the Carthaginians, they could hardly come to the aid of Saguntum. Whatever, the Romans claimed

9 In 226 BC Hasdrubal, diplomat rather than a soldier, had signed the Iber Treaty with Rome, which defined areas of influence in the Iberian Peninsula by preventing the Carthaginians from crossing the river Iber (Ebro) under arms (Polybios 2.13.7).

Relief (Madrid, museo arqueológico nacional) from Osuna, Seville, depicting an Iberian warrior wearing a short linen tunic, usually white with crimson borders, and wielding a short, but deadly sword, the *falcata*, a curved single-bladed weapon derived from the Greek *kopis*. He carries a flat, oval body shield. (Author's collection)

that the alliance with this town overrode the treaty, and the Carthaginians claimed that the same agreement allowed them to attack Saguntum (Polybios 3.21.1, 29.1–3, 30.3).

Polybios pulls no punches, for he has an unambiguous view that the Saguntum episode was a mere pretext. As he had earlier pointed out to his readers, those Roman historians who have tried to identify the causes of the war between Rome and Carthage with the Carthaginian action in laying siege to Saguntum and the subsequent crossing of the Iber have got it all wrong. What he does concede, however, is that 'these events might be described as the *beginnings* of the war' (3.6.2).

Hannibal's aims

Hannibal's long-term objective was fairly straightforward. From his father Hamilcar Barca he had learnt that is was inadvisable to be bogged down in a slogging match with Rome. If Polybios (2.24) is to be believed, Rome and its allies had a manpower resource of some 700,000 infantry and 70,000 cavalry. No matter how many times Hannibal knocked out a Roman army, another would stubbornly take its place. Hannibal, knowing that over half of Rome's forces were furnished by its allies, deliberately set out to strangle this supply of manpower by claiming Italy would be freed from the Roman yoke. It is for this reason that he had to invade Italy, as distant rumours of Punic victories would not convince Rome's allies to switch sides.

Iberian horse, who were of excellent quality and what Polybios classes as 'bridled cavalry' (3.65.6), were trained and equipped to fight *en masse*. Although badly worn, this relief (Madrid, museo arqueológico nacional) from Osuna, Seville, clearly shows a horseman armed with a curved sword. (Author's collection)

Terracotta plaque (Paris, musée du Louvre, 5223) from southern Italy depicting a mortally wounded Numidian horseman. Riding without either bridle or saddlecloth almost from infancy, Numidians rode small, swift horses that appeared scrawny but were capable of enduring where heavier mounts could not. (Author's collection)

The execution of the objective was, on the other hand, far from simple. Hannibal could invade Italy from the sea, a much faster and easier task than crossing the Alps. However, without bases in Sicily, even southern Italy was at the limit of operational range for a fleet of oared warships operating from Africa, and Punic naval power in Iberia was not great. Another stumbling block to this option was Rome's superior naval strength, 220 quinqueremes to Carthage's 105 (Polybios 3.33.4, 41.2, Livy 21.49.2, 4). And so, with Carthage outmatched, and perhaps outclassed, on the high seas, the risk of a seaborne invasion was too great a one for Hannibal to take. The next logical step, especially if you are based in Iberia, is to invade via southern Gaul, and thus Hannibal needed to march over the Alps.

It is almost certain that Hannibal did not envisage a final triumph amongst the smoking ruins of a sacked Rome. Polybios (3.77.3–7, 85.1–4) clearly shows him releasing his Latin and Italian prisoners of war without ransom money having been demanded of them. Livy (22.58.1–2) also has Hannibal continuing this policy after Cannae, adding that Hannibal addressed his Roman prisoners and stressed that he was not fighting to destroy them, but 'for honour and empire' (22.58.3). Though he may have sworn eternal hatred of them, Hannibal was not planning to exterminate the Romans. Two facts support this hypothesis. First, Hannibal, after Cannae, attempted to negotiate with Rome. Second, a clause in the treaty between Philip V of Macedon and Carthage shows Rome being stripped of its allies but allowed to exist as a simple Latin city (Polybios 7.9.12–15). Hannibal's aim was to defeat Rome's armies and thereby force it to the negotiating table, where it would be then stripped of its allies and burdened with a crippling war indemnity. With Rome reduced to the status of a second-rate power, Carthage would have been able to regain Sicily, Sardinia and its other lost territories, as well as having a free hand in Iberia.

The long struggle

The Senate's plan for the conduct of the war was simple and direct. The consuls were to operate separately: one was to go to Iberia to face Hannibal, whilst the other was to go to Sicily to prepare an invasion of Africa (Polybios 3.40.1–2, 41.2, Livy 21.17.1–9). To the utter surprise and consternation of the Romans, Hannibal marched over the Alps during the late autumn of 218 BC. He then proceeded to defeat one Roman army after another in a series of three brilliant victories: the Trebbia (Polybios 3.70–74, Livy 21.54–56), Trasimene (Polybios 3.82–84, Livy 22.4–6), and Cannae (Polybios 3.111–17, Livy 22.46–49).

The immediate result of these Roman disasters was that most of southern Italy came over to Hannibal, a series of events that started with the defection of Capua (216 BC), the capital of Campania and second only to Rome itself in size and prosperity, and culminates in the betrayal of Tarentum (212 BC). Though the citadel still remained in the hands of the small Roman garrison, the capture of Tarentum gave Hannibal access to a major port. Meanwhile the Carthaginian senate negotiated an alliance with Philip V of Macedon (215 BC) and the conflict spread into Sicily, where Syracuse broke its alliance with Rome and went over to Carthage (214 BC). This diplomatic coup was regarded as a real danger to Rome and the continued existence of its hegemony in Italy, as the Carthaginians could now use Sicily as a convenient stepping-stone into the peninsula. Rome, therefore, rapidly despatched an army to recapture Syracuse, which, despite the fabulous efforts of the local genius Archimedes, was duly

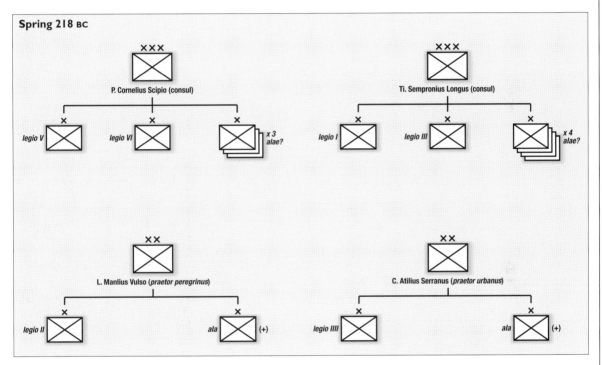

The Senate's initial strategy was not to fight a defensive war; rather it planned an aggressive opening to the war where one consular army, under P. Cornelius Scipio, would be sent to Iberia and another, under Ti. Sempronius Longus, to Africa via Sicily (Polybios 3.40.2, 41.2, Livy 21.17.5, 8). The speed of Hannibal's advance from the Iber to the Po Valley derailed the Roman pincer strategy.

Having failed to intercept Hannibal at the Rhône, Scipio sent his elder brother Cnaeus (cos. 222 BC), who was serving as his deputy, on to Iberia as planned with his consular army. Scipio himself hurried back to Italy to take command of the two legions recently sent to Gallia Cisalpina, one under the *praetor peregrinus* L. Manlius Vulso, and the other under the *praetor urbanus* C. Atilius Serranus (Polybios 3.49.1–4, 56.5–6, Livy 21.26.2, 32.1–5). One of these legions is designated *legio IIII* by Polybios (3.40.14) and the other was probably *legio II*, originally levied for Scipio's Iberian expedition too. Meanwhile Sempronius was recalled from Sicily with his consular army and ordered to join Scipio in defending Italy (Polybios 3.61.7–9, Livy 21.51.5). The Senate had thus raised six legions for the year.

P. Cornelius Scipio (consular army) Two replacement *legiones* (*V* and *VI*), supported by 14,000 allied infantry and 1,600 allied cavalry (three *alae?*): despatched to Iberia under Cn. Cornelius Scipio Calvus

Ti. Sempronius Longus (consular army) Two *legiones* (*I* and *III*), supported by 16,000 allied infantry and 1,800 allied cavalry (four *alae?*): originally earmarked for Africa, but redirected to Gallia Cisalpina

L. Manlius Vulso & C. Atilius Serranus (two praetorian armies) Two ex-consular *legiones* (*II* and *IIII*), supported by two reinforced Latin-Italian *alae* (10,000 allied foot, 1,000 allied horse): despatched to Gallia Cisalpina but later under P. Cornelius Scipio

subdued (212 BC). This event, and the recapture of Capua (211 BC) despite Hannibal's march on Rome itself to divert the besiegers, are seen as the turning points in the war.

Of course it is all very well in hindsight to pinpoint a crucial year when events turned in favour of Rome. Lest we forget, for instance, the year 211 BC also witnesses the crushing defeat, by Hasdrubal son of Gisgo and Hannibal's brothers Hasdrubal and Mago, of the two Roman armies operating in Iberia, the commanders, Cn. Cornelius Scipio Calvus and P. Cornelius Scipio, losing their lives to boot (Livy 25.32–36). They had stalwartly maintained the struggle in

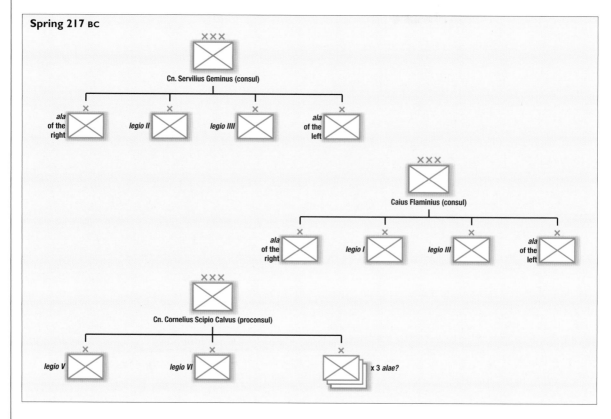

Spring 217 BC

Cn. Servilius Geminus (consul)

ala of the right — legio II — legio IIII — ala of the left

Caius Flaminius (consul)

ala of the right — legio I — legio III — ala of the left

Cn. Cornelius Scipio Calvus (proconsul)

legio V — legio VI — x 3 alae?

The new consuls marched north, Caius Flaminius to Arretium (Arezzo) and Cn. Servilius Geminus to Ariminum (Rimini), in an attempt to cut Hannibal off from the most obvious routes into central Italy (Polybios 3.77.1–2, 80.1, 86.1, Livy 22.2.1, 4). We do not have a detailed breakdown of the citizens and allies levied this year, but the consuls both seem to have been given the standard consular army of two legions and two *alae*, composed of a mixture of newly raised troops (Polybios 3.75.5) and the remnants of the consular armies defeated at the Trebbia (Livy 21.63.1, Appian *Hannibalic War* 8). Geminus' army is said to have included at least 4,000 cavalry, probably allies in the main (Polybios 3.86.3, Livy 22.8.1).

The troops commanded by the two consuls, however, were not the only forces put into the field by Rome this year. There were already two legions, with allied contingents, serving in Iberia under Cn. Cornelius Scipio Calvus, and Polybios says (3.75.4) legions were despatched to Sicily and Sardinia after the Trebbia. On the basis of Livy's evidence for their numbers in future years Lazenby (1978: 61) assumes that two were sent to Sicily and one to Sardinia. Finally, Brunt (1971: 648) suggests that the practice of levying two 'city legions' (*legiones urbanae*) each year, to act as a garrison for the city of Rome (*Urbs Roma*), began this year. If so, this means that the Senate had raised 11 legions, five more than the previous year and a striking demonstration of Rome's immense manpower resources.

Cn. Servilius Geminus (consular army) Two *legiones* (II and IIII), supported by two Latin-Italian *alae* with 3,400 allied cavalry: Gallia Cisalpina

Caius Flaminius (consular army) Two *legiones* (I and III), supported by two Latin-Italian *alae*: Etruria

Cn. Cornelius Scipio Calvus (ex-consular army) Two *legiones* (V and VI), supported by 14,000 allied infantry and 1,600 allied cavalry (three *alae*?): Iberia

Plus *legiones* in Sicily (2), Sardinia (1), Rome (2)

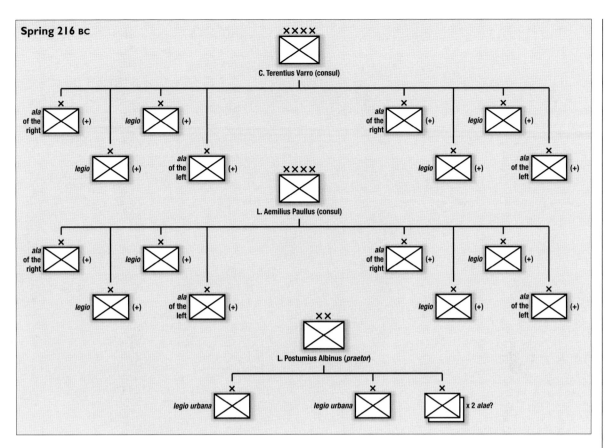

Spring 216 BC

C. Terentius Varro (consul)
ala of the right (+) | legio (+)
legio (+) | ala of the left (+)
ala of the right (+) | legio (+)
legio (+) | ala of the left (+)

L. Aemilius Paullus (consul)
ala of the right (+) | legio (+)
legio (+) | ala of the left (+)
ala of the right (+) | legio (+)
legio (+) | ala of the left (+)

L. Postumius Albinus (praetor)
legio urbana | legio urbana | x 2 alae?

The Senate decided to raise eight legions, a double-sized army of four legions for each consul, 'a step which', observes Polybios, 'the Romans had never taken before' (3.107.9, cf. Livy 22.36.2–4). Furthermore, as both consuls were expected to fight together, the Senate's objective was clear: to seek battle with Hannibal's army and destroy it. Not only were there more legions than usual, but also each legion was increased in size to 5,000 legionaries as well as the usual complement of 300 citizen-horsemen (Polybios 3.107.9–11). In all between 15 and 17 legions were in service by the summer of 216 BC, a total of perhaps 75,000 to 80,000 men, around a quarter of the number of citizens Polybios says (2.24) were eligible for service in 225 BC. Supporting these were a similar number of allied infantry, whilst the allied cavalry was more numerous.

Assuming that Polybios is correct, and Appian (Hannibalic War 17) supports him here, half of the eight Cannae legions had been newly raised (spring 216 BC) and the other four were the legionaries formerly commanded by the dictator Q. Fabius Maximus Cunctator. These consisted of two legions raised by Fabius to replace those lost at Trasimene (Livy 22.11.2–3, cf. Polybios 3.88.8), and two legions formerly commanded by Cn. Servilius Geminus. As consul Servilius had taken command in March 217 BC of half the army, which had reformed after the Trebbia. His colleague Caius Flaminius took over the two legions (I and III) commanded by Ti. Sempronius Longus and Servilius took those of P. Cornelius Scipio (Livy 21.63.1, Appian Hannibalic War 8). Both of these legions (II and IIII), originally raised for Scipio's expedition to Iberia, had been despatched to Gallia Cisalpina in 218 BC when the Boii rebelled, one under the praetor peregrinus L. Manlius Vulso, the other under the praetor urbanus C. Atilius Serranus (Polybios 3.40.14, 49.1–4, 56.5–6, Livy 21.26.2, 32.1–5). It is assumed that these existing four legions were brought up to the same strength as the four new ones, raising the same number of allied infantry, man for man, and three allied cavalryman for every two Roman.

This was not the only Roman Army to be fielded in this year. In addition to the forces in Iberia and Sicily, two legions apiece, and one legion in Sardinia, a double-praetorian army was sent north to face the tribes of Gallia Cisalpina, which remained in open rebellion. Under the command of the praetor L. Postumius Albinus (cos. I 234 BC, cos. II 229 BC), the two legions that composed this army were possibly the legiones urbanae raised by the consuls at the beginning of the year (Polybios 3.106.6, Livy 23.14.2).

C. Terentius Varro (double-consular army) Four reinforced legiones, each of 5,000 legionaries and 300 equites, supported by four reinforced Latin-Italian alae with 1,800 allied cavalry: Apulia

L. Aemilius Paullus (double-consular army) Four reinforced legiones, each of 5.000 legionaries and 300 equites, supported by four reinforced Latin-Italian alae with 1,800 allied cavalry: Apulia

L. Postumius Albinus (double-praetorian army) Two legiones, possibly the legiones urbanae, supported by similar number of allied troops (two alae?): Gallia Cisalpina

Plus legiones in Iberia (2), Sicily (2), Sardinia (1)

Shekel (London, British Museum) showing the elephant regularly employed by the Carthaginians. The African forest elephant (*Loxodanta africana cyclotis*) was smaller than the Indian species – 2.15 to 2.45m tall at the shoulder it carried a single rider, not a howdah – but was easier to train than today's African bush elephant. (Author's collection)

Iberia for eight long years, and when Cicero later referred to the brothers as the 'thunderbolts of our empire' (*Pro Balbo* 34) he presumably was thinking of their brief glory, followed by sudden extinction. Though many senators were probably inclined to abandon Iberia, the Senate despatched a new commander to this distant theatre, the young P. Cornelius Scipio (Africanus), the son and nephew of the dead Scipiones, who, after five years of hard fighting, drove the Carthaginians out of Iberia and eventually invaded Africa via Sicily.

Two years later, exhausted but not rebellious, 12 of the 30 Latin colonies declared themselves incapable of providing further soldiers and resources for the war effort (Livy 27.9.7–14). In 207 BC the sudden arrival of Hasdrubal Barca in northern Italy caused panic and despair in Rome; we can only speculate at what would have happened if the two Barca brothers had combined forces. Hasdrubal himself was certainly no second-rate general by any stretch of the imagination, and this is one of those spectacles that grab our attention because the 'might have been' seems so nearly realized. Thus, by contemporary standards, it was not Syracuse and Capua that saw the turning point in the war, but the Metaurus.

And so the decisive year is 207 BC when Hasdrubal suffered defeat, and death, at the river Metaurus in Umbria (Polybios 11.1–3, Livy 27.47–49). Having managed to extricate his army out of Iberia following the reverse at Baecula (Bailén) at the hands of the younger Scipio, Hasdrubal decided 'to march to Italy to share the fortunes of his brother Hannibal' (Polybios 10.37.5). Fortunately for Rome, however, its two consuls, M. Livius Salinator and C. Claudius Nero, joined forces and consequently crushed this bold attempt to reach southern Italy. The first news that Hannibal received of the fate of his reinforcements was his brother's head, carefully preserved, thrown into his

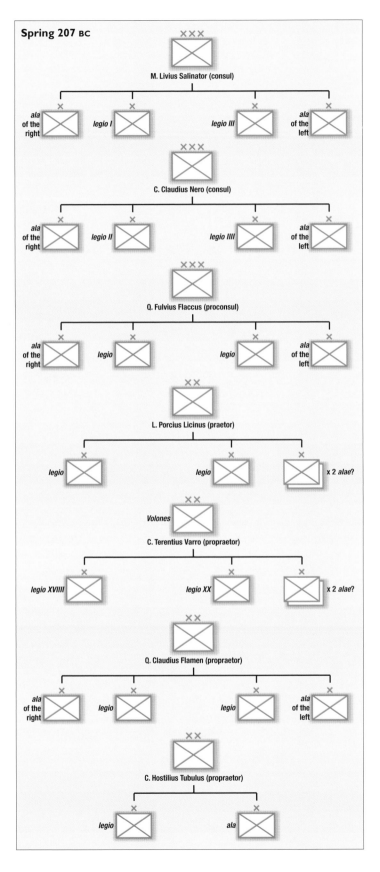

Spring 207 BC

M. Livius Salinator (consul)

ala of the right | legio I | legio III | ala of the left

C. Claudius Nero (consul)

ala of the right | legio II | legio IIII | ala of the left

Q. Fulvius Flaccus (proconsul)

ala of the right | legio | legio | ala of the left

L. Porcius Licinus (praetor)

legio | legio | x 2 alae?

Volones
C. Terentius Varro (propraetor)

legio XVIIII | legio XX | x 2 alae?

Q. Claudius Flamen (propraetor)

ala of the right | legio | legio | ala of the left

C. Hostilius Tubulus (propraetor)

legio | ala

The news that another son of Hamilcar Barca was set to invade Italy with fire and sword caused panic in Rome. One of the consuls, M. Livius Salinator (cos. I 219 BC), was sent north with a consular army. He was supported by one of the praetors, L. Porcius Licinus, who commanded 'two weak legions' (Livy 27.39.2) based near Ariminum (Rimini), whilst C. Terentius Varro (cos. 216 BC) led a similarly sized force on the other side of the Apennines in Etruria. The latter Livy (28.10.11) describes as being composed of the *volones*, slaves he had previously mentioned (22.57.11) as having volunteered to serve in the army after Cannae, disbanded in 211 BC. This means that Varro's two units were *legiones XVIIII* and *XX* into which the *volones* had been drafted (Livy 27.38.10).

The other consul, C. Claudius Nero, was sent to lead the ring of armies containing Hannibal in the south. As well as his own consular army of two legions with their normal complement of allied troops, Nero could call upon two legions under the proconsul Q. Fulvius Flaccus (cos. I 237 BC, cos. II 224 BC, cos. III 212 BC, cos. IV 209 BC) in Bruttium, two legions under the propraetor Q. Claudius Flamen in the region of Tarentum, and the legion at Capua under the propraetor C. Hostilius Tubulus. Thus, with the two new *legiones urbanae* raised this year, bringing the total in service to 23 legions, no fewer than 15 legions were concentrated in the Italian peninsula, nearly four times the number that had faced Hannibal in 218 BC. The other eight legions were operating in Iberia, Sicily and Sardinia (Livy 27.36.10–13).

M. Livius Salinator (consular army)
Two *legiones* (*I* and *III*), supported by two Latin-Italian *alae*: Gallia Cisalpina

C. Claudius Nero (consular army)
Two *legiones* (*II* and *IIII*), supported by two Latin-Italian *alae*: Apulia

Q. Fulvius Flaccus (ex-consular army)
Two *legiones*, supported by two Latin-Italian *alae*: Bruttium

L. Porcius Licinus (double-praetorian army) Two under-strength *legiones*, supported by similar number of allied troops (two *alae*?): Gallia Cisalpina

C. Terentius Varro (*volones* army)
Two under-strength *legiones* (*XVIIII* and *XX*), supported by similar number of allied troops (two *alae*?): Etruria

Q. Claudius Flamen (double-praetorian army) Two *legiones*, supported by two Latin-Italian *alae*: Apulia

C. Hostilius Tubulus (praetorian army)
One *legio*, supported by one Latin-Italian *ala*: Campania

Plus *legiones* in Iberia (4), Sicily (2), Sardinia (2)

M. Claudius Marcellus (d. 208 BC)
In 208 BC the stage was set for the first full-scale confrontation with Hannibal since Cannae. But before battle was joined, the consuls were ambushed near Venusia by a band of Numidians, M. Claudius Marcellus being killed, and T. Quinctius Crispinus mortally wounded (Polybios 10.32.1–6, cf. Livy 27.26.7–11). Marcellus (cos. I 222 BC, cos. II 214 BC, cos. III 210 BC, cos. IV 208 BC) had fought with distinction during the closing stages of the First Punic War, and was awarded the *corona civica* for saving his brother's life in battle. Arguably the best soldier Rome apparently possessed, of Marcellus Hannibal apparently said that he 'is the only general who when victorious allows the enemy no rest, and when defeated takes none himself' (Plutarch *Marcellus* 9.4). Though obviously not in Hannibal's league as a commander, he was a veteran fighter who was never laid low by defeat and served Rome well, especially in the dark days after Cannae.

Marcellus was certainly far more aggressive than his contemporary, Q. Fabius Maximus Cunctator. During his first consulship he had killed the Insubrian king, Britomarus, in single combat and stripped him of his armour. This heroic deed had won for him the highest honour available to a Roman aristocrat, the right to dedicate the third and the last *spolia opima* ('spoils of honour') to Iuppiter Feretrius, and his ensuing victory over the Gauls that day earned him a triumph (Plutarch *Marcellus* 6-8, *Fasti Triumphales* 531 AUC). During the middle Republic about one consul in three celebrated a triumph, but it was not an inaccessible honour like the *spolia opima*, the name given to the spoils taken in personal conflict by a Roman general from the general of the enemy. The second occasion was when A. Cornelius Cossus slew Lars Tolumnius, the Etruscan king, and carried off the *spolia opima* (428 BC), which was the first won since the victory of the hero-king, Romulus (Livy 1.10, 4.19–20). It was commonly said that Fabius was the shield, while Marcellus was 'the sword of Rome' (Plutarch *Marcellus* 9.4), a fitting tribute for this hero-general.

camp by the Romans. 'Now, at last, I see the destiny of Carthage plain', Hannibal is said to have mourned (Livy 27.51.12). According to Ovid, 'Hasdrubal fell by his own sword' (*Fasti* 6.770), and although Hasdrubal is not said to have committed suicide, it is quite clear that he deliberately sought death in battle when he realized that all was lost. Having done all that a good general should, as Polybios (11.2.1) emphasizes, Hasdrubal died in the thick of the fighting, sword in hand.

Hannibal was finally isolated in southern Italy and, three years later, he and his younger brother Mago received the summons to return to Carthage. He had maintained himself in a hostile land for 15 years, during which time he continued to shower defeats on one consular army after another. In addition to the disasters already mentioned, as the years went by the armies of Ti. Sempronius Gracchus (212 BC), M. Centenius Paenula (212 BC), Cn. Fulvius Centumalus Maximus (210 BC) and M. Claudius Marcellus (208 BC) went

C. Claudius Nero
C. Claudius Nero (cos. 207 BC) had been one of M. Claudius Marcellus' officers in the scrambling fights with Hannibal around Canusium (209 BC). Previous to that, both as praetor (212 BC) and propraetor (211 BC), he had been one of the successful commanders at the siege of Capua, before being sent temporarily to Iberia after the deaths of the elder Scipiones. He was thus a soldier of experience, and although Livy declares (27.34.2) that he had a somewhat ambiguous reputation for boldness verging on rashness, he was to turn out one of the best Roman generals of the war.

Taking the pick of the citizen and allied troops in his consular army, some 6,000 foot and 1,000 horse, he led them north to join his fellow-consul, M. Livius Salinator (Livy 27.43.6–12). In this desperate campaign, Nero showed himself to be a general infinitely better than Hasdrubal, and even better than Hannibal, for his bold manoeuvre was a triumph not just for discipline and determination, but for the logistical organization that allowed him to arrange in a matter of days for supplies to be prepared in advance along his route. Likewise, his decision to march from the right wing to outflank the enemy on the opposite end of the battlefield displayed a degree of tactical flexibility unimaginable at the beginning of the war (Polybios 11.1.7). Horace (*Odes* 4.4) describes the day of the battle of the Metaurus as the first on which victory smiled on the Romans since Hannibal had crossed the Alps.

Salinator was awarded a triumph for this decisive victory, the first allowed to any general in this war, and Nero, who had been his subordinate, the lesser honour of an ovation (*ovatio*). However, Livy claims that when Nero rode on horseback behind Salinator's four-horse chariot the cheers were louder for him, the crowd believing that he had been the real architect of the victory. By archaic tradition Roman soldiers who marched in a triumph sang ribald verses at their commander's expense. Nero received the slightly dubious honour of being the target of more of these jibes than his senior colleague (Livy 28.9.2–20).

down like ninepins before Hannibal, and the Roman generals were killed. With Scipio now operating in Africa a peace treaty was tentatively agreed, but the negotiations were soon terminated and the final showdown between Hannibal and Scipio was played out at Zama in 202 BC (Polybios 15.9–14, Livy 30.32–35).

With its defeat Carthage became a 'friend of Rome', losing all its overseas possessions and most of its African lands, surrendering all elephants – and no more to be trained according to Livy (30.37.3) – and reducing its once proud navy to a mere ten triremes, as well as agreeing to a war indemnity of 10,000 Euboian talents of silver to be paid in 50 yearly instalments. In addition, Carthage was not allowed to conduct war in Africa without the prior approval of Rome (Polybios 15.18.5–10). The time span of 50 years was obviously intended to prolong the period of subjection and prevent the paying off of the indemnity in advance.

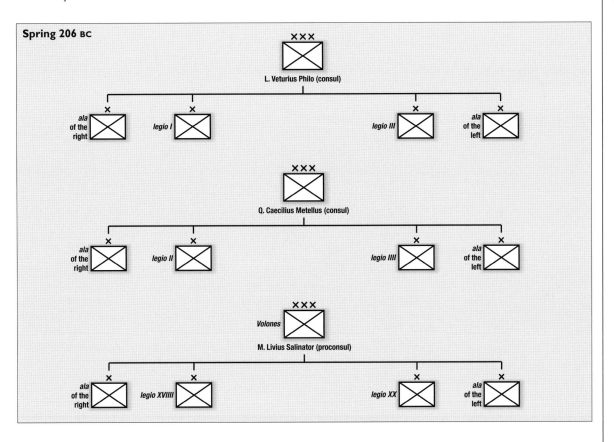

M. Livius Salinator's (cos. I 219 BC, cos. II 207 BC) *imperium* was prorogued, and he took command of *legiones XVIIII* and *XX*, presumably still under strength, which C. Terentius Varro (cos. 216 BC) had previously commanded in Etruria. The rest of the dispositions made by the Senate were much the same as for the previous year (see above, page 67), except that both consuls, L. Veturius Philo and Q. Caecilius Metellus, were assigned to Bruttium (Livy 28.10.8), each with a consular army of two legions with their normal complement of allied troops, and that one of the new praetors, Q. Mamilius Turrinus, was to take over the army of L. Porcius Licinus, and carry out reprisals against the Gallic tribes that had aided Hasdrubal (Livy 28.10.12). The total number of legions was, however, reduced from 23 to 20, the two legions that had garrisoned Sardinia for a number of years being brought home and disbanded, and replaced by a single legion (Livy 28.10.14). Salinator's consular army was also disbanded, presumably as a reward for its part in the victory at the Metaurus.

L. Veturius Philo (consular army) Two *legiones* (*I* and *III*), supported by two Latin-Italian *alae*: Bruttium

Q. Caecilius Metellus (consular army) Two *legiones* (*II* and *IIII*), supported by two Latin-Italian *alae*: Bruttium

M. Livius Salinator (*volones* army) Two under-strength *legiones* (*XVIIII* and *XX*), supported by two Latin-Italian *alae*: Etruria

Plus *legiones* in Iberia (4), Sicily (2), Sardinia (1)

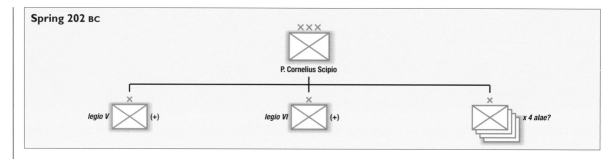

Spring 202 BC

XXX
P. Cornelius Scipio

legio V (+)   *legio VI* (+)   x 4 alae?

According to Livy the survivors of Cannae were sent to Sicily where they made up two legions (*legiones Cannenses*). Later reinforced by the survivors of the first battle of Herdonea (211 BC), these disgraced troops were not to be released from service and were forbidden to return to Italy until the war was over (Livy 25.5.10. 26.1.9–10). Ironically, as Livy remarks (29.24.13), these penal soldiers became the most experienced troops in the entire Roman Army, P. Cornelius Scipio (Africanus) consequently making them the backbone of his the African expeditionary force (204 BC). Renumbered as *legiones V* and *VI*, Livy says (29.24.14) these were exceptionally strong units of 6,200 infantry with the usual complement of 300 citizen-cavalry.

The actual size of the invasion force is unknown. Livy mentions (29.25.1–4) three different totals given by unnamed sources, ranging from 10,000 foot and 2,200 horse, through 16,000 foot and 1,600 horse, to a maximum of 35,000 for both arms. It is assumed here that the middle totals represent the number of infantry and cavalry furnished by the socii.

P. Cornelius Scipio (pro-consular army) Two 'strong' *legiones* (V and VI), each of 6,200 legionaries and 300 *equites*, supported by 16,000 allied infantry and 1,600 allied cavalry (four *alae*?): Africa

The Trebbia, genius at work

For military historians, the battle of the Trebbia suitably illustrates the many facets of Hannibal's military genius. Here they can witness his psychological insight into the minds of his Roman opponents, his concern for the welfare of his own men, his willingness to try the unexpected and his ability to use each element of his army to the best advantage within the parameters of a simple battle plan. It is also the only major battle, apart from Zama, in which he used elephants.

The land west of the Trebbia is wide, flat and treeless, yet Hannibal, during a personal reconnaissance, had located a watercourse crossing the open plain and running between two steep and heavily overgrown banks. Lying behind and south of where he expected to lure the Romans to fight a pitched battle, it was in and among the scrub and other vegetation of this natural feature that he set an ambush under the command of his young brother Mago (Polybios 3.71.9). The day before the expected encounter a picked force of 1,000 infantry and 1,000 cavalry, mostly Numidian, was formed for this vital task. Under the cover of darkness Mago inserted his men into the ambush position, where they were completely hidden from the view of the Romans. The stage was thus set for the first major confrontation in the Hannibalic War.

At first light the following morning – Polybios says (3.72.3) the day was near the winter solstice – Hannibal's Numidian horsemen mounted and crossed the river to skirmish around the Roman outposts and provoke Ti. Sempronius Longus into premature action, while the rest of the Carthaginian Army stayed by their campfires to eat a hearty breakfast and rub their bodies with olive oil to keep out the biting cold (Polybios 3.72.6, Livy 21.55.1). Sempronius reacted just as Hannibal had hoped, sending all his cavalry out against the audacious Numidians, closely followed by some 6,000 *velites*. The consul, eager to engage, then gave orders for his infantry to stand to arms and prepare to march out against the enemy, thereby giving them little or no time to take their morning meal. At this point the raiders, following their strict instructions, began to give way and gradually retire toward the river. The bait had been taken.

When the Romans proceeded to cross the river, ice-cold and swollen breast-high by recent rain, Hannibal threw forward 8,000 light-armed troops to support

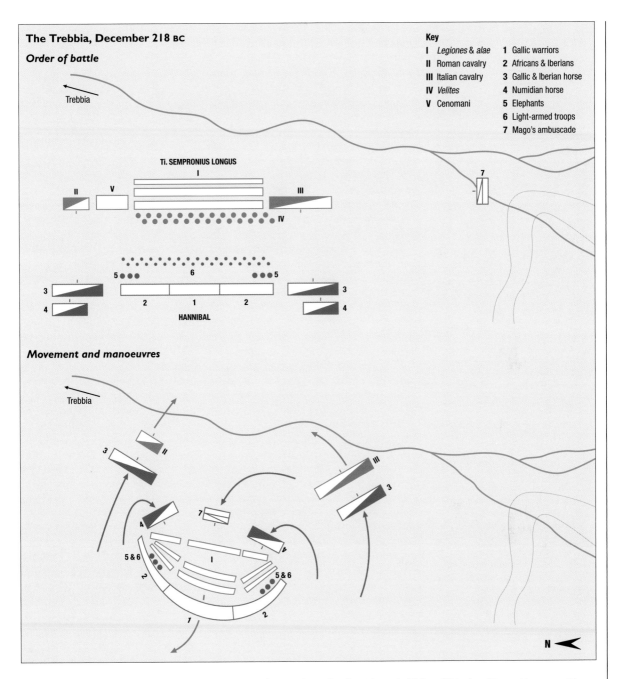

The Trebbia, December 218 BC

Order of battle

Trebbia

Key

I	*Legiones & alae*	1	Gallic warriors
II	Roman cavalry	2	Africans & Iberians
III	Italian cavalry	3	Gallic & Iberian horse
IV	*Velites*	4	Numidian horse
V	Cenomani	5	Elephants
		6	Light-armed troops
		7	Mago's ambuscade

Ti. SEMPRONIUS LONGUS

HANNIBAL

Movement and manoeuvres

Trebbia

N

Hannibal had come over the Alps to Gallia Cisalpina, won a large-scale cavalry skirmish on the Ticinus (Ticino), and in a cold, snowy mid-December was camped on the west bank of the Trebbia close to its confluence with the Po, south-west of Placentia (Piacenza). On the other bank of the river were the consuls, Ti. Sempronius Longus and P. Cornelius Scipio, with four legions (*I* to *IIII*) and, perhaps, six Latin-Italian *alae*. They also had the support of the Cenomani, the only Gallic tribe in northern Italy to remain loyal. Scipio was recovering from a severe wound and *hors de combat*, but his colleague was all out for giving battle and Hannibal was aware of this. So he set out deliberately to lure Sempronius into a trap on the flat, open terrain between the two camps.

Order of battle
Polybios says (3.72.11–13) the Roman Army contained 16,000 Roman and 20,000 allied foot, and 4,000 cavalry, while Livy (21.55.4) adds a contingent (of doubtful value) from the Cenomani. Scipo's wound obliged him to pass the command over to Sempronius. If the figures given for Hannibal's army are correct, and if Mago's 2,000 men are to be added to the total, the Carthaginian Army had been swelled by over 14,000 Gauls – 9,000 foot and 5,000 horse – for Hannibal had entered the Italian Peninsula with only 20,000 infantry – Africans and Iberians – and 6,000 Iberian and Numidian cavalry (Polybios 3.56.4). He also commanded 30 or so elephants, having started his epic journey with 37 of these rather risky weapons.

the Numidians and form a screen behind which his army could deploy. Then, and only then, his main body left the camp and advanced a little over a kilometre (Polybios 3.72.8), where they fell into a line of battle. This took the form of a single line of close order infantry, 20,000 strong, with his new Gallic allies in the centre, and his 10,000 cavalry, including the rallied Numidians, equally divided on each flank. Hannibal also divided his elephants, and probably stationed them in front of the two wings of his infantry line (Polybios 3.72.9, cf. Livy 21.55.2).

Having struggled across the river, Sempronius deployed his infantry, now half frozen, soaked and very hungry, in the customary three-line formation, with the 4,000 cavalry, now recalled from their fruitless pursuit of the Numidians, and the Cenomani on their flanks (Polybios 3.72.11, Livy 21.55.4). During what must have been a long, drawn-out process, more so as the army was uncommonly large and relatively inexperienced, the snow of the early morning turned to driving sleet and rain.

The battle opened with the usual exchanges between the skirmishers of both sides, and here the Romans were soon at a disadvantage. Not only were the *velites* outnumbered, but they had already been engaged with Hannibal's Numidian horsemen and thus expended much of their missile supply. After a short engagement, therefore, they fell back through the intervals between the maniples, and Sempronius, who remained full of confidence, ordered a general advance. At this point, Hannibal, taking advantage of his superiority in this particular arm, let loose his cavalry.

The citizen and allied cavalry, heavily outnumbered and already worn down from chasing the agile Numidians, gave way at the first shock of these fresh troops, broke and fled in rout for the river, with the Iberian and Gallic horse in merciless pursuit. The Numidians coming up behind, however, at once swung inwards upon the exposed flanks of the Roman infantry just as the elephants and light-armed troops similarly engaged them.

The Roman infantry, despite their cold and hunger, had managed to hold their own with Hannibal's infantry and might have prevailed. Then the elephants, in cooperation with the light-armed troops, began to attack the Roman centre. It was at this point that Mago, timing his attack to a nicety, sprung his ambush and charged into the Roman rear. Then, at last, Sempronius' army began to break up (Polybios 3.74.1). Still, some 10,000 infantry in the centre of the first and second lines, refusing to accept defeat, hacked their way through the Gauls who made up Hannibal's centre. Then, seeing all was lost and that a return across the swollen river to their camp was completely cut off, they marched off in good order and made their escape to the walls of Placentia. Hannibal made no attempt to stop them. His men were weary and his victory was assured.

Though we do not have a figure for the Roman losses, the rest of the Roman Army must have suffered heavily in the rout towards the river. Likewise, the sources are vague for Hannibal's casualties, although Polybios says (3.74.11) that the Gauls in the centre suffered the heaviest losses. However, in the cold snap that followed the battle, many of his men and horses and all but one of the elephants died.

Lake Trasimene, the perfect ambush

Hannibal had lost the sight of an eye while travelling through the wetlands around the river Arno. By then he had also lost almost all his elephants. Yet Hannibal, the consummate trickster, had never envisaged a decisive role for elephants in his cunning battle-plans. And so at Lake Trasimene in Etruria, his one eye still clear sighted enough to outwit another Roman consul and his army, Hannibal made use of a novel ruse. For his troops, hidden in the dawn mist from the lake and the marshy vegetation, unexpectedly fell on the flank and rear of the Roman Army. The battle was an ambush on the grand scale, one of those rare

Flaminius broke camp at Arretium and pressed post haste after Hannibal along the road from Cortona to Perusia. At the north-western angle of Lake Trasimene, seen here from Fortezza di Girifalco Cortona, he made camp intending to pursue his march along the northern shore the next day. (Author's collection)

instances in the annals of military history in which a whole army lies in wait and accounts for almost the whole of the opposition. Hannibal commanded roughly 55,000 men, of which 20,000 were seasoned veterans and 25,000 recruits from the anti-Roman Gauls in Gallia Cisalpina (Polybios 3.33.11, 72.9).

At dawn Caius Flaminius had set out after his apparent prey, in thick mist, with no apparent attempt at reconnaissance (Polybios 3.84.1). On seeing the African and Iberian outposts, the doomed Roman Army began to form up for the attack, only to be completely surprised by the rest of the Carthaginian Army charging downhill out of the clinging white veil into their flanks and rear. From the moment that the ambush was sprung Hannibal's victory was certain. Unable to organize any effective resistance, most of the Romans were cut down while they were still in marching order, some even drowning in the quiet waters of the lake as they tried to flee. Here too, the consul was slain, by 'a band of Celts' according to Polybios (3.84.6), by a horse-warrior of the Insubres named Ducarius according to Livy (22.6.1–4), who recognized Flaminius as the man responsible for the earlier defeat of his people (223 BC). The vanguard, some 6,000 Romans, cut its way out, only to be surrounded and captured the next day.

Polybios says (3.84.7) 15,000 Romans died in the misty valley, but this was probably the total of all who were killed, as Livy (22.7.2), citing the

Hannibal's spectacular ambush and defeat of Flaminius' army took place somewhere along the northern shore of Lake Trasimene, seen here from Castiglione del Lago By entering the narrow space between the hillside and the water, the unsuspecting Romans were doomed from the very outset. (Author's collection)

On the road from Arretium (Arezzo) to Perusia (Perugia) Hannibal had trailed his coat before the consul Caius Flaminius, who commanded a standard consular army of about 20,000 men, before disappearing into a narrow defile north of Lake Trasimene (Largo Trasimeno). The arena itself was a natural amphitheatre bounded on all sides by hills or water, a perfect killing ground for an unsuspecting foe. This certainly fits well with the description given by Polybios of 'a flat-bottomed valley having on its long hill and continuous hills, in front a barren, steep crest and in its rear the lake' (3.83.1).

Order of battle

Hannibal set the stage with care. He placed his African, namely Libyan and Libyphoenician, and Iberian veterans on the ridge blocking the exit from the killing ground, where they would be in plain view of the advancing Romans. His light troops, with the Gallic horse, were hidden from view behind the crest of the hills on his left, the Gallic warriors similarly hidden in folds in the ground running down to the defile, and the Carthaginian cavalry, Iberians in the main, and Numidian horse near the entrance where they could block it off once the Romans had passed through (Polybios 3.83.2–4). Dispositions made, the army settled down for the night.

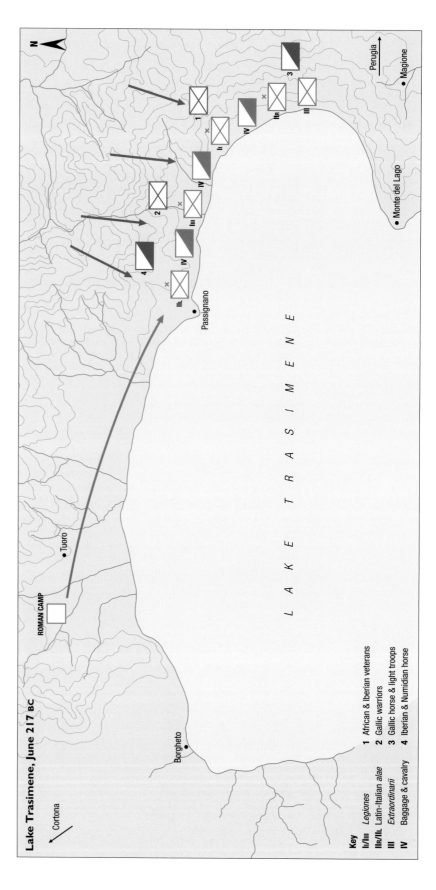

Lake Trasimene, June 217 BC

Key
II/III *Legiones*
IIₐ/IIₗ Latin-Italian *alae*
III *Extraordinarii*
IV Baggage & cavalry

1 African & Iberian veterans
2 Gallic warriors
3 Gallic horse & light troops
4 Iberian & Numidian horse

contemporary account of Q. Fabius Pictor, makes clear, and Polybios' total of 15,000 prisoners (3.85.2) is probably also too high. Hannibal's losses were some 1,500 in all, according to Polybios (3.85.5) most of them Celts; Livy says (22.7.3) 2,500 were killed in battle, and many more died later of their wounds.

Cannae, a lesson in annihilation

Military historians regard this battle as a classic example of a successful double-envelopment manoeuvre, and Cannae, still studied in Western military academies, is a lesson in annihilation striven after by many military commanders. For instance, Count Alfred von Schlieffen, the architect of the plan used for the German invasion of France in August 1914, was obsessed with Hannibal's victory, studying the battle time and time again for inspiration as he painstakingly drafted and re-drafted his grand design. The resultant plan bore only a superficial similarity to Hannibal's tactics at Cannae and was conceived on an infinitely grander scale. It also failed.

Being faced by a vastly more numerous force Hannibal decided, in effect, to use the very strength of the enemy infantry to defeat it, deliberately inviting it to press home its attack on the centre of his line. His African veterans would serve as the jaws of the trap, the Gallic and Iberian warriors as the bait. Finally, Hannibal took equal care with the deployment of his cavalry; it too would play an integral part in the entrapment of the Romans. Instead of distributing his cavalry equally between the wings, he placed more cavalry on the left against the river there. This virtually guaranteed a breakthrough against the numerically far inferior Roman cavalry, and it would then be available for further manoeuvres. The smaller body of cavalry on the open flank, away from the river, where the more numerous Italian cavalry was stationed, would be expected to hold them in play for as long as possible. The Carthaginian dispositions at Cannae, made in full view of the enemy and on a treeless space, actually constituted an ambush. Not only was this a beautifully thought-out, audacious scheme, but it showed Hannibal's absolute confidence in the fighting abilities of all the contingents of his army.

The Roman legions, supported by the allied *alae*, were drawn up in their customary three lines behind a forward screen of skirmishers. However, not only were the maniples deployed closer together than usual but their frontage was reduced and their depth increased (Polybios 3.113.3). The Roman tactics were to try and smash through the Punic line by sheer weight of numbers as had happened at the Trebbia (Polybios 3.74.3). With this reversion to the principle of sheer mass, flexibility and manoeuvrability were renounced and the rigidity of the phalanx was reinstated. Commanding the centre was

---

C. Terentius Varro

The consular elections of 216 BC were held amid scenes of savage bickering and popular demand for strong measures against the Punic invaders (Livy 22.33.9–34.1). It is therefore no surprise that when the first elections were finally held, the sole candidate to be elected was C. Terentius Varro, a strong advocate of meeting Hannibal in battle.

Varro's subsequent defeat has made him the scapegoat of most ancient writers, who have eagerly seized upon suggestions that he was a gutter demagogue, a butcher's son and a dangerous fool (Livy 22.25.18–26.4, Plutarch *Fabius Maximus* 14, Appian

Hannibalic War 17, Dio fr. 57.24). These writers have chosen ignore the Roman senatorial system and have not bothered to investigate Varro's previous career too closely. As Lazenby (1978: 74) rightly remarks, it would have been impossible for a butcher's son to be elected to the consulship, and the worst that can be said of Varro in this respect is that he was a *novus homo* rather than from an old established *gens*.

He had in fact already served as quaestor (222 BC), aedile (221 BC) and praetor (218 BC), and thus had climbed the established career ladder, the *cursus honorum*. Like all those seeking political careers, Varro would have first served

in the army at the age of 17. It is also possible that Varro had seen active service in Illyria (219 BC). The picture we are usually given of the vain, arrogant bully who could harangue a meeting but not command an army is therefore somewhat wide of the mark. It would seem that Varro, while certainly no military genius, was no worse a commander than his predecessors, notably the unconventional Caius Flaminius. However, Livy (22.61.15) was quite right to point out that if Varro had been Carthaginian, he would probably have been crucified. Yet even after the catastrophic defeat at Cannae, he subsequently commanded an army in Etruria (208 BC, 207 BC).

Military historians regard Cannae as a classic example of a successful double-envelopment manoeuvre. On this hot, dusty, treeless plain, by withdrawing his centre while the wings stood firm, Hannibal annihilated some 50,000 Romans after they were lured forward into the jaws of the Punic Army. (Author's collection)

Regulus, the consul *suffectus* of 217 BC, and Servilius, Flaminius' original colleague (Polybios 3.114.6, cf. Livy 22.40.6). The 2,400 citizen-cavalry was stationed on the right flank by the Aufidus and commanded by the consul Paullus, whilst his colleague Varro, who was also in overall command, took charge of the left with the 3,600 allied cavalry.

Meanwhile the Carthaginian centre formed up in a single convex line, also screened to its front by skirmishers, composed of the Gallic and Iberian war-bands (Polybios 3.113.8–9). Hannibal himself, with his brother Mago, took up position here. The African veterans, divided into two phalanxes – the hoplite rather than the Macedonian version (Polybios 1.33.6, 34.6) – were deployed on the wings of this thin crescent-shaped line. However, now dressed and armed with equipment stripped from the dead of the Trebbia and Lake Trasimene, they looked for the entire world like Roman legionaries (Polybios 3.87.3, 114.1, Livy 22.46.4). Hannibal's Gallic and Iberian horse, probably 6,500 strong and led by Hasdrubal (one of Hannibal's Carthaginian lieutenants), was stationed on his left wing by the Aufidus, the Numidians on his right, led by either Hanno son of Bomilcar (Polybios 3.114.7) or Maharbal son of Himilco (Livy 22.46.7, 51.2).

Hannibal launched the Gallic and Iberian horse head-on – the latter were certainly trained and equipped to fight en masse (Polybios 3.65.6) – thereby routing the heavily outnumbered Roman cavalry. Instead of being dissipated in useless pursuit, the victors swung behind the advancing Roman juggernaut to fall on the rear of the Italian cavalry, who had been held in play by the skirmishing Numidian horse. The legionaries gradually pushed back the Gallic and Iberian war-bands, but avoided the Africans, who swung inwards to attack the flanks. The Gallic and Iberian horse left the Numidians to pursue the now fleeing Italian cavalry, and fell on the rear of the legionaries, thus drawing pressure off the Gallic and Iberian warriors and effectively surrounding the Roman centre. This, the final phase of the battle, was not to be an affair of tactical sophistication, but of prolonged butchery. The eventual outcome was a massacre and, in Livy's dramatic rhetoric, the carnage was 'a shocking spectacle even to an enemy's eyes' (22.51.5).

In a single day some 48,200 Romans were killed (Livy 22.49.15, cf. Polybios 3.117.2–4), 4,500 captured on the battlefield (Livy 22.49.18), with 14,200 taken elsewhere (Livy 22.49.13, 50.11, 52.4, cf. Polybios 3.117.7–11). One proconsul, namely Servilius, two quaestors, 29 military tribunes, a number of ex-consuls, praetors and aediles, and 80 senators, also perished with the army (Livy 22.49.16). Of the consuls, Paullus was killed and Varro fled from the field (Polybios 3.116.12, 16). Of the Carthaginians, some 8,000 'of his [Hannibal's] bravest men' (Livy 22.52.6, cf. Polybios 3.117.6) were killed.

The Metaurus, the beginning of the end

After tumbling out of the Apennines, for the last leg of its journey the Metaurus meanders through a wide, gently shelving valley into the Adriatic. At the time the land either side of the wide river was probably thickly wooded, restricting vision and movement so as to make the Metaurus a confusing obstacle, uncertain in its course and inaccessible over much of its length.

On learning that M. Livius Salinator and L. Porcius Licinus had been joined by C. Claudius Nero, Hasdrubal left his campfires burning and quietly slipped away under the cover of darkness. His intention may have been to retreat across the Apennines into Etruria. Having been abandoned by his two guides, presumably local men, he gave orders to follow the river bank until it was light enough to find the way, intending to cross the Metaurus as soon as a suitable place to do so was located. It was an unfortunate decision.

The weary column soon became confused by the winding turns of the river and made little progress. As dawn broke the Carthaginians found themselves overtaken by the enemy cavalry (Livy 27.47.10–11). Once the Romans had concentrated, they formed into line with Salinator on the left, Licinus in the centre, and Nero on the right, apparently with his own infantry and cavalry. It is unclear from our sources whether all the cavalry were divided between the left and right wings, as was the usual practice, although Livy seems to imply that the bulk of the citizen-cavalry were with Salinator on the left, which may mean Nero had the allied cavalry. At the first appearance of the Romans, Hasdrubal had started to prepare a fortified camp on a hill overlooking the river, but seeing that a battle was unavoidably imminent he ordered his exhausted troops to deploy (Livy 27.48.1–3).

Hasdrubal put the Gauls on the left, where a steep, difficult ravine protected them. These were the least reliable part of his army, many of them having deserted during the arduous night march, while others apparently slept during the encounter being inebriated – in the aftermath of the battle they were to be butchered in their beds 'like sacrificial victims' (Polybios 11.3.1). The centre of the battle line was made up of the recently recruited Ligurians (only mentioned in Livy's account), the right wing of veteran Iberian warriors. Because of the confined space and haste of deployment, the army was drawn up in depth and on a narrow front. Hasdrubal's ten elephants – 15 according to Appian (*Hannibalic War* 52) – were posted either in front of the Ligurians or the Iberians (Polybios 11.1.5–6, cf. Livy 27.48.4–7). As Hasdrubal attacked with his faithful Iberians, hoping to win the battle by smashing the Roman left, it seems reasonable to assume that the elephants were actually posted to their front.

Initially there was desperately hard but fairly even fighting, the elephants getting out of hand and doing as much damage to friend as to foe. But Nero, unable to come to grips with the Gauls opposite him and guessing the obstacle to his front would also prevent them from advancing, boldly marched round behind the Roman ranks and fell on the open flank and rear of the Iberian warriors. These were almost wiped out, and the rest of the army suffered heavily as Nero rolled up the Punic line (Polybios 11.1.7–10). Hasdrubal himself, when he saw all was lost, deliberately charged into the thick of the slaughter and fell sword in hand.

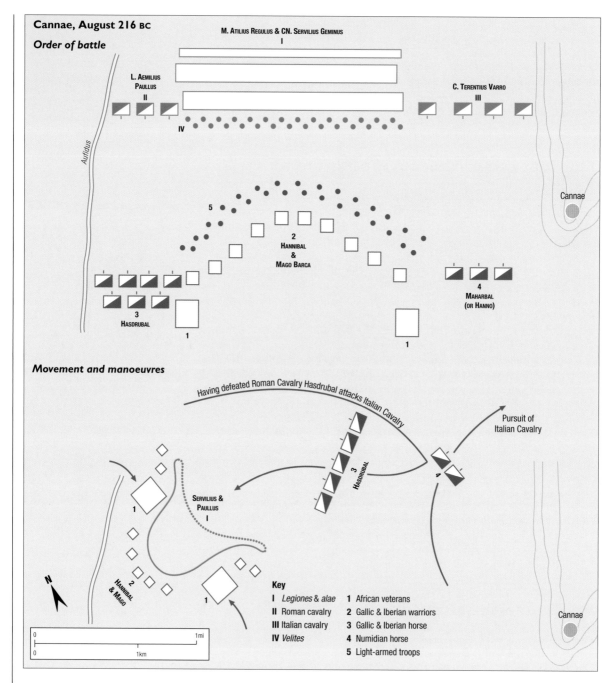

Cannae, August 216 BC

Order of battle

M. ATILIUS REGULUS & CN. SERVILIUS GEMINUS
I

L. AEMILIUS PAULLUS
II

C. TERENTIUS VARRO
III

IV

Aufidus

5

2
HANNIBAL
&
MAGO BARCA

3
HASDRUBAL

1

4
MAHARBAL
(OR HANNO)

1

Cannae

Movement and manoeuvres

Having defeated Roman Cavalry Hasdrubal attacks Italian Cavalry

Pursuit of Italian Cavalry

3
HASDRUBAL

4

SERVILIUS & PAULLUS
I

1

2
HANNIBAL & MAGO

1

N

Cannae

0   1mi
0   1km

Key

I	*Legiones & alae*	1 African veterans
II	Roman cavalry	2 Gallic & Iberian warriors
III	Italian cavalry	3 Gallic & Iberian horse
IV	*Velites*	4 Numidian horse
		5 Light-armed troops

The town of Cannae (Canne della Battaglia), Apulia, lay on the right bank of the Aufidus (Ofanto) some 8km from the Adriatic Sea, the hill upon which it sat being the last spur of generally rising ground in that direction. Below Cannae the river runs through mainly flat, treeless country, but that on the left bank is noticeably more so than that on the right. The left bank, in fact, is perfect cavalry country, never exceeding the 20m contour throughout the whole area between Cannae and the sea, whereas on the right bank, though the ground is mostly level, it rises slowly but steadily from the sea to reach the ridge by Cannae. However, although some authorities have placed the battle on the left bank, it is an easier reading of our best sources to locate the fighting on the right bank, assuming the river's course originally lay further away from the hill of Cannae itself (Lazenby 1978: 77–79, Goldsworthy 2000B: 201, 2001: 86–93, Daly 2002: 32–35).

Order of battle
Eight reinforced *legiones* and eight reinforced Latin-Italian *alae* totalling 80,000 infantry and 6,000 cavalry under the two consuls, C. Terentius Varro and L. Aemilius Paullus, with the consuls of the preceding year, M. Atilius Regulus and Cn. Servilius Geminus, also present (Polybios 3.113.5, 114.6). Hannibal commanded about 40,000 infantry – Africans (Libyans, Libyphoenicians), Iberians and Gauls – and 10,000 Iberian, Gallic and Numidian cavalry (Polybios 3.114.6).

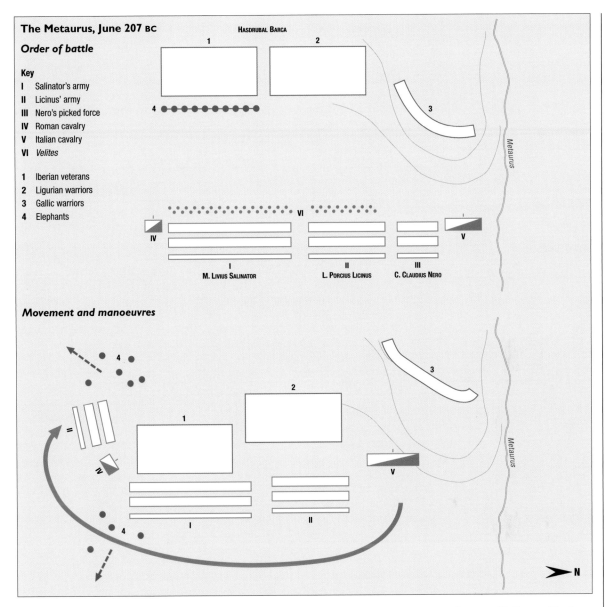

The Metaurus, June 207 BC

Order of battle

HASDRUBAL BARCA

Key

I Salinator's army
II Licinus' army
III Nero's picked force
IV Roman cavalry
V Italian cavalry
VI *Velites*

1 Iberian veterans
2 Ligurian warriors
3 Gallic warriors
4 Elephants

I — M. LIVIUS SALINATOR
II — L. PORCIUS LICINUS
III — C. CLAUDIUS NERO

Movement and manoeuvres

N

Despite his defeat in a rearguard action at Baecula (Bailén), Hasdrubal Barca had skilfully extricated his small army and led it out of Iberia. He then swiftly marched across the Alps into Gallia Cisalpina, according to Livy and Appian by the same route that Hannibal had followed 11 years previously, but without encountering any of the same difficulties or opposition. After delaying before Placentia, which was probably to enable him to recruit the Cisalpine Gauls and Ligurians who now joined him, Hasdrubal finally moved south-eastwards, pushing the army of L. Porcius Licinus before him. At some point, the consul M. Livius Salinator joined Licinus. The other consul, C. Claudius Nero, who was shadowing Hannibal in the south, had the good fortune to intercept Hasdrubal's sealed letters to his brother. Realizing the danger, he decided, with the pick of his army, to slip away and make a dash north to join his colleague at Sena Gallica (Senigallia) about 400km up the Adriatic coast. It was a decision that was to give him his place in history.

Order of battle

The numbers for this battle are a matter of guess work. According to Polybios (11.3.2), no fewer than 10,000 Carthaginians (Iberians mostly) and Gauls fell in the battle, for the loss of 2,000 Romans. Six elephants were killed along with their mahouts, and the other four rounded up in the aftermath (Polybios 11.1.11). From Livy (27.49.6) we learn, despite his grossly inflated figure of 56,000 for the Carthaginian losses, that there were 5,400 prisoners. In addition, some of Hasdrubal's men must have escaped, and some may have not reached the battlefield at all if we are to believe Livy (27.47.9). Hasdrubal's army would thus appear to have been between 20,000 and 30,000 strong. Salinator's army was a full consular army of two *legiones* (I and III) supported by two Latin-Italian *alae*, totalling perhaps 20,000 or so men, and while Licinus also had two *legiones*, presumably supported by the usual allied contingent, his double-praetorian army was specifically described as 'weak' (Livy 27.39.2), and may not have mustered more than 15,000 men. The Roman force, however, was reinforced by Nero's picked force of 6,000 infantry and 1,000 cavalry.

Ilipa, Iberia lost

The fate that had overtaken the armies of his father and uncle had taught P. Cornelius Scipio (Africanus) not to rely overmuch upon his Iberian allies. However, as the infantry of the Roman legions and the Latin-Italian *alae* on their own could not hope to defeat the numbers mustered by Hasdrubal son of Gisgo, Scipio needed to devise a tactical plan whereby he would use the Iberian warriors to threaten and mislead the enemy, but leave the real fighting to his own troops.

For a few days the rival armies deployed to offer battle in the plain between their respective camps, but neither advanced far enough to force the issue, contenting themselves instead with sporadic skirmishing (Polybios 11.21.7). Each day Hasdrubal placed his Africans in the centre and his Iberian allies, along with the elephants, on the wings. Scipio followed the customary Roman practice, putting his legions and *alae* in the centre and his own Iberian allies on either side.

One day, his men having already partaken of an early breakfast, Scipio led his army out of camp and formed up for battle in the grey light of dawn. This time, however, he placed his legions and *alae* on the wings and the Iberians in the centre (Polybios 11.22.6). Hasdrubal, taken completely by surprise, had to deploy for battle in great haste, his troops forsaking their morning meal as they hurried to take up their normal positions. By the time Hasdrubal realized that the Romans had changed their accustomed dispositions, it was too late.

Scipio ordered a general advance. Next he wheeled his legions and *alae* off in column away from the centre, which was ordered to advance very slowly towards the enemy battle line. Here it is of interest to note the actual words used by Polybios to describe Scipio's complicated manoeuvre, for he says Scipio took 'three maniples – this unit of infantry is called a "cohort" among the Romans – wheeling them to the left on the right, and to the right on the left' (11.23.2). The remark about the three maniples being called a 'cohort' becomes clear if we remember that in battle a legion was customary ranged in three lines, or *triplex acies*. Thus when the lines wheeled into column to left and right, the columns would have been led by a maniple each of *hastati*, *principes* and *triarii*. In the distant future, as we well know, the cohort of three maniples would become the standard tactical unit of the legion. Anyhow, back at Ilipa Scipio's two columns of infantry, right and left wings, then turned at right angles towards the Carthaginians, and finally deployed obliquely to cover the gaps between them and the still advancing centre.

The citizen and allied cavalry, and the *velites*, had remained on the outer flanks of the legions and *alae* throughout the elaborate manoeuvre, and now emerged to fall on the flanks of the Carthaginian Army, while the infantry assaulted Hasdrubal's Iberian allies (Polybios 11.23.3–6). Hasdrubal's veteran Africans, facing the Roman centre, which had contrived not to come into contact, could only watch while the legions and *alae* did their work.

The first to suffer were the elephants. Galled by the missiles of the cavalry and *velites*, they soon got out of hand. Wheeling round, they blundered back, thereby doing as much damage to their own side as to the enemy (Polybios 11.24.1). The whole Punic line fell into utter confusion and broke up as individuals raced for the safety of their camp, only to be saved from total destruction by a violent thunderstorm (Polybios 11.24.8).

It was Hasdrubal's intention on the following day to hold firm in his camp, but the bulk of his Iberian warriors, feeling no doubt that they had been left to bear the brunt of the fighting, began to desert in droves. Understandably Hasdrubal ordered a retreat, but Scipio was alert. During the ensuing hot pursuit, according to Livy (28.16.1–6), Hasdrubal himself escaped with a bare 6,000 men into the neighbouring hills.

Hasdrubal along with Mago and the Numidian prince Masinissa, eventually managed to take refuge in the stronghold of Gades (Cadiz), but Ilipa and its aftermath sealed the doom of the Punic Empire in Iberia. It also demonstrated that the seasoned army led by Scipio, who had been present both at the Trebbia and Cannae, had a far higher standard of training and corporate discipline than Roman armies had possessed in the early years of the Hannibalic War. His outflanking move in the very face of the enemy is probably the most complex manoeuvre attempted by a Roman army to date, and for the student of military history shows the manoeuvrability and flexibility of the manipular legion at its best.

Zama, a lesson learnt

The Romans were naturally horrified when the news reached them of the defeat at Cannae and its scale. First reports made no mention of survivors, and the Senate was told that the entire army had been simply annihilated. Not until 14 years later, when Roman troops were in Africa, was Rome to exact its revenge. Having invaded Africa, the brilliant young Scipio turned the tables and Hannibal was decisively defeated near the small town of Zama. Without the resources or will to continue the struggle, Carthage sued for peace and the Second Punic War was over.

Hannibal deployed his army in three lines mirroring the Roman formation. The first line was composed of Ligurians, Gauls, Balearic slingers and some Mauri, and appears to be the remnants of Mago Barca's mercenaries brought back from Italy. Polybios says (15.11.1) there was 12,000 infantry in this line. The second line consisted of Punic, Libyphoenician and Libyan

P. Cornelius Scipio Africanus (236–185 BC)
The Carthaginians lost because Rome, with its huge reserves of high-quality manpower, refused to admit defeat even when it was down on its knees. Second, central Italy and its colonies did not revolt and the Gauls, as a nation, did not join Hannibal (or his brother Hasdrubal). Third, Carthage failed to gain the command of the sea and dissipated its war effort. Fourth,

the Cornelii Scipiones confined Hasdrubal Barca to Iberia until 208 BC, and produced in the younger P. Cornelius Scipio (cos. I 205 BC, cos. II 194 BC), who would later celebrate a triumph and take the cognomen 'Africanus', a soldier whose tactical genius was at least equal to that of Hannibal's.

Of course we have to remember the Cornelii Scipiones were one of the most influential of Roman families, and very much a law unto themselves. We only have to think of the way the future Scipio Africanus secured the command in Iberia, vacant after the deaths of his father and uncle in 211 BC, despite being a private citizen (*privatus*) and never having held any office higher than that of aedile. The aedile was a middle-ranking magistrate without military duties, being solely responsible for maintaining roads and aqueducts, supervising traffic and markets, and organizing public games and festivals.

Scipio was an inspiring leader who could gain and keep the loyalty of his men. His charismatic character and judicious diplomacy won him many allies, without whom Rome might have not won the war. Seeing the deficiencies of the rather static traditional Roman tactics, Scipio

experimented with small tactical units that could operate with greater flexibility. His tactics were inspired by Hannibal's and needed good legionary officers as well as generalship to implement. He thus saw the value of capable subordinates who could proceed on their own initiative.

Scipio's strategy of striking at Punic forces in Iberia, and letting the conquest of ground take care of itself, was brilliant, and was in complete contrast to that of his predecessors. But although he has been extravagantly praised for his strategy of invading Africa, this had been the Roman plan since 218 BC, and appears pedestrian in comparison with Hannibal's daring invasion of Italy and rapid succession of victories. Both men were fine tacticians but Ilipa, Scipio's most tactically sophisticated battle, appears ponderous when compared with Cannae. Hannibal himself is supposed to have said that, if he had won Zama, he would have rated himself even better than Alexander the Great (Livy 35.14.9). That is debatable, but few would agree with Suvorov that Scipio was the better general, even though he won that particular battle. Hannibal was beaten, not by a better man, but by a better army. Great soldier as Scipio was, he falls short of the rank attained by Hannibal.

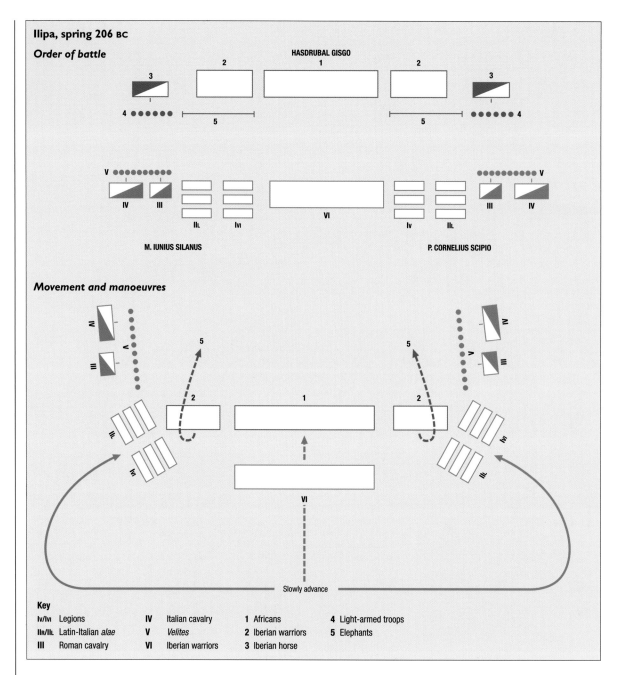

Ilipa, spring 206 BC

Order of battle

HASDRUBAL GISGO

Movement and manoeuvres

M. IUNIUS SILANUS

P. CORNELIUS SCIPIO

Slowly advance

Key

Iv/Ivi	Legions	IV	Italian cavalry	1	Africans	4	Light-armed troops
IIR/IIL	Latin-Italian *alae*	V	*Velites*	2	Iberian warriors	5	Elephants
III	Roman cavalry	VI	Iberian warriors	3	Iberian horse		

News of the disaster on the Metaurus had no doubt reached Iberia, and Hasdrubal son of Gisgo now decided to make a final great effort to expel the Romans from the peninsula. Having gathered the remaining Punic forces in Iberia, Hasdrubal left his winter quarters at Gades (Cadiz) and marched north, concentrating near the town of Ilipa (Alcalá del Rio), which lay on the right bank of the Baetis (Guadalquivir) some 14km north of modern Seville (Polybios 11.20.1, Livy 28.12.15, cf. Appian *Iberica* 25). Meanwhile, P. Cornelius Scipio (Africanus) advanced up the Baetis and encamped opposite him.

Order of battle

Hasdrubal, together with Mago Barca, had succeeded in raising an army estimated by Polybios (11.20.2) at 70,000 infantry and 4,000 cavalry, and by Livy (28.12.14) at about 50,000 infantry and 4,500 cavalry. He also had supporting elephants, 32 according to Polybios (11.20.2), 36 according to Appian (*Iberica* 25). As for the army of Scipio, which he seems to have commanded since 210 BC, only just over half were Roman or Italians, the two *legiones* (V and VI) and two *alae* composing the standard consular-sized army. The remainder were auxiliary troops, many recently recruited from Rome's new allies amongst the Iberian tribes and somewhat similar to the warriors whose desertion had precipitated the disaster suffered by his father and uncle. In total he mustered around 45,000 infantry and 3,000 cavalry (Polybios 11.20.8, cf. Livy 28.13.5).

Zama, October 202 BC

Order of battle

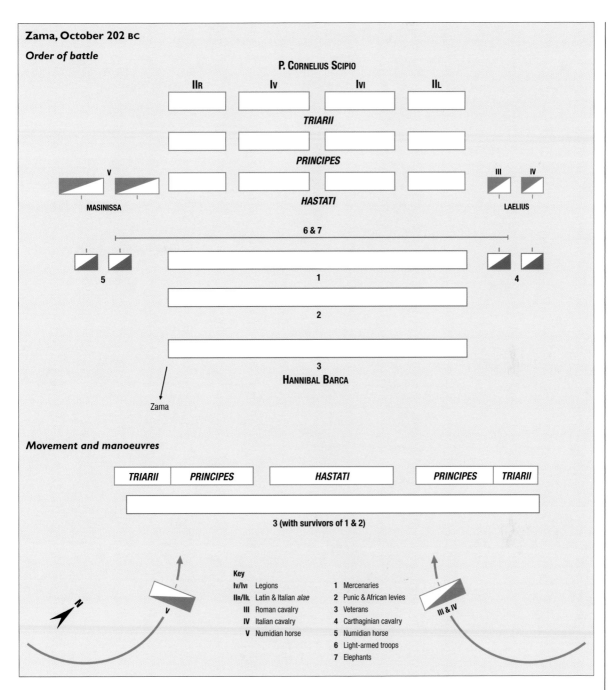

Movement and manoeuvres

From the neighbourhood of Hadrumetum (Sousse), Hannibal marched his army to a place Polybios calls Zama, 'a town which lies about five days' march to the west [i.e. south-west] of Carthage' (15.5.3). Of the four places called Zama in ancient Tunisia, the one referred to here has been identified as the one that lay at Seba Biar, some 13km east of Zanfour (Lazenby 1978: 218). Between the two camps the two commanders met for their famous parley (Polybios 15.6.1–8.14, Livy 30.29.1–10, cf. Frontinus *Strategemata* 1.1.3, 6.2.1, 2), and it was on the second day, at dawn, that the armies deployed for battle. In keeping with his view of the importance of Zama in shaping the course of world history, Polybios says, with unaccustomed drama, that 'the Carthaginians were fighting for their very survival and the possession of Africa, the Romans for the empire and the sovereignty of the world' (15.9.2).

Order of battle

Hannibal probably commanded some 36,000 infantry, supported by 4,000 cavalry, half of them Numidian, and 80 elephants (Polybios 15.3.6, 11.1, 14.9). Appian (*History of Libya* 41) gives Scipio 23,000 Roman and Italian foot and 1,500 horse. His infantry included the two penal legions, now designated *legiones V* and *VI*, formed from the survivors of Cannae (*legiones Cannenses*). Masinissa brought with him a force of 6,000 foot and 4,000 horse (Polybios 15.5.12, Livy 30.29.4).

levies raised for the defence of Africa. The third line, some distance behind the others and in reserve, consisted of Hannibal's own veterans, that is, the soldiers who had come with him from Italy (Polybios 15.11.2). Livy (30.33.6) and Appian (*History of Libya* 40) make these predominantly Bruttii, but they clearly included all the survivors of his Italian army, even some Africans and Iberians who had marched with him from Iberia and the Gauls who had joined him in Gallia Cisalpina. Polybios clearly says (15.11.7–9) that Hannibal, in a pre-battle address, told his veterans to remember above all the victories they had gained over the Romans at the Trebbia, Lake Trasimene and Cannae, and later Polybios emphasizes that these men were 'the most warlike and the steadiest of his fighting troops' (15.16.4). The cavalry was positioned on either wing, the Carthaginians (Punic, Libyphoenician) on the right and the Numidians on the left, with the elephants and light-armed troops in front of the infantry (Polybios 15.11.1). For the first time in his career, Hannibal was fighting on ground not of his choosing and with inferiority in the mounted arm.

During his campaign in Iberia Scipio had struck up a friendship with a most useful prince in Numidia, Masinissa, and on African soil his brilliant horsemen would prove crucial allies. Scipio stationed Masinissa with his Numidian contingent on the right wing, and his lieutenant, Caius Laelius, with the citizen and allied cavalry on the left wing. In the centre the Roman infantry were drawn up with the maniples of *hastati*, *principes* and *triarii* one behind the other, thus leaving lanes to accommodate the elephants. All his *velites* were stationed in the lanes with orders to fall back in front of the elephants or, if that proved difficult, to right and left between the lines (Polybios 15.9.7–10).

In the event, a large proportion of the elephants, being young and untrained, were frightened out to the wings where they did more harm to their own side than to Scipio's, thereby helping his cavalry to sweep their counterparts from the field (Polybios 15.12.2–5). The infantry then closed and after the *hastati*, supported by the *principes*, had broken the first two Punic lines, Scipio redeployed his second and third lines on either wing of the first.

Splendid triple-disc cuirass (Tunis, musée de Bardo) from a tomb at Ksour-es-Sad, Tunisia. This was probably taken back to Africa by one of Hannibal's veterans, perhaps an Oscan-speaking warrior who fought (and survived) at Zama. A broad bronze belt, the symbol of manhood, would accompany this armour. (Author's collection)

Readjustments made, he then closed with Hannibal's veterans who were also probably now flanked by the survivors from their first two lines as Polybios says (15.14.6) the two forces were nearly equal in numbers. The struggle ended when the Roman cavalry and Numidian horse returned and fell on Hannibal's rear. The mercenaries and levies turned and fled, Hannibal escaped with a small escort, but his hard-nosed veterans, largely armed and equipped in the Roman style, fought bitterly to the death, pitted against those very legionaries that they had disgraced at Cannae. Polybios (15.14.9) assesses the Carthaginian casualties as 20,000 dead and 20,000 prisoners, the Romans losing no more than 1,500 men.

Polybios concludes his account of the battle with the view that Hannibal had done all that a good general of long experience should had done, 'brave man as he was, he met another better' (15.6.6, quoting *Iliad* 4.300). Scipio adopted the cognomen 'Africanus' by virtue of his achievement, the first Roman general to be known by a name derived from the scene of his victories.

Military superpower

After the crushingly one-sided success at Cannae, says Livy, Maharbal boasted to his victorious commander-in-chief that he, at the head of the cavalry, could ride to Rome where Hannibal should be 'dining, in triumph, on the Capitol within five days' (22.51.5). Hannibal, although he commends his cavalry commander's zeal, demurs. Maharbal retorts by saying that Hannibal knew how to win a fight, but did not know how use the victory. 'This day's delay,' Livy piously concludes, 'is generally believed to have been the salvation of the city and the empire' (22.51.6).

Rome was 400km away, a distance that would take at least three weeks to cover with the army marching at a forced rate of 20km a day, ample time for the Romans to organize the defence of the city. Moreover, Rome still had two legions sitting within the city itself, and a fleet stationed at Ostia, which raised a legion of marines after Cannae (Livy 22.57.7–8). It must also be remembered that the Roman Army was a citizen force; the population of Rome could be armed easily and by this means defend the walls of their city. Besides, if Hannibal had galloped away from southern Italy he would have left an area that was offering him vital support in his struggle with Rome. No part of Hannibal's long-term strategy involved a march on Rome, and even in 211 BC, when he stood at its gates, he was simply tempting the Romans to lift their siege of Capua.

Like Livy, Polybios' special concern was with Rome. Unlike the moralizing Livy, however, his prime object was to explain to horrified fellow-Greeks 'by what means and under what kind of constitution the Romans in less than 53 years succeeded in subjecting the whole inhabited world to their sole government' (1.1.5). For Polybios (1.3.7, 15.9.2–4, cf. 5.104.4–10) Rome's victory at Zama was the turning point in its history. Of the 53-year period (220–167 BC) he covers in his near-contemporary account of the unification of the known world under the guidance and control of Rome, the Second Punic War dominates a third. When, in 211 BC, Hannibal did stand outside the gates of Rome, his achievement was not to be repeated until Alaric the Visigoth pillaged the 'eternal city' in AD 410. Among its enemies Rome's chief *bête noire* was undoubtedly Hannibal, and '*Hannibal ad portas*' retained its efficacy as a rallying cry for Romans in times of national crisis until the end of the empire. The crux is, before the war Rome was predominately an Italian power, but now, however, its armies had marched through southern Gaul, Iberia, Sardinia, Corsica, Sicily, Africa and Illyria. Rome's range and ambitions had been transformed.

The Hannibalic War had also revealed the latent power of Rome, that is, its capacity to produce men. Most of Rome's previous wars had been fought with two consular armies each of two legions and their usual complement of allied contingents, and Polybios says (3.107.9) that when eight legions were mobilized for the Cannae campaign, this had never before been done. But if Polybios is right in stating there were eight legions at Cannae, Rome had already mobilized a total of ten legions, since there were already two in Iberia, and by 211 BC there were 25 legions in the field, which, taking the allied contingents and the men serving at sea into consideration, represented something like 250,000 men (Brunt 1971: 419–422). As Cineas, the trusted diplomat of King Pyrrhos, was said to have predicted, the many-headed monster could regenerate and struggle on (Plutarch *Pyrrhos* 19.7).

This inexhaustible supply of manpower is an obvious reason as to why Rome finally defeated Hannibal. At Cannae Rome lost, according to Livy

(22.49.15), nearly 50,000 troops, namely the army had suffered 80 per cent casualties. The casualty rate suffered by Britain and its colonial allies during the first day of the Somme in 1916 does not compare with this shocking figure (19,240 killed, 35,493 wounded, 2,152 posted as missing and 585 captured). No other state in antiquity could have survived such a shattering defeat. Rome also had a solid core of support amongst its closest dependencies, the Latin communities, despite a bout of war-weariness at Rome's endless calls on their manpower, and even those 12 that had refused to supply troops never opted to side with Hannibal. With northern and central Italy refusing to back Hannibal, his long-term strategy was not going to be a success. The evidence from negotiations between the defectors (mainly Samnites, Rome's traditional foes) and Hannibal shows that what they really wanted was autonomy and the chance to determine their own fate. Defection to Hannibal, who was after all an outsider, was changing one master for another, or so many feared.

Chronology

During their official year, which was named after them, the two consuls were all-powerful and irremovable. The consular year usually began on the Ides of March and as a result the consuls remained in office for the first few months of the year after the date given below. Numerals in brackets after a name denote whether the man held the consulship before. As the First Punic War progressed the number of men holding office for the second time increased, which may have provided more experienced commanders. Likewise for the Second Punic War.

Date	Consuls	Events
264 BC	Ap. Claudius Caudex	Rome accepts appeal of Mamertini
	M. Fulvius Flaccus	
263 BC	M'. Valerius Maximus Messala	Hieron II allies Syracuse with Rome
	M'. Otacilius Crassus	
262 BC	L. Postumius Megellus	Siege of Agrigentum
	Q. Mamilius Vitullus	
261 BC	L. Valerius Flaccus	Fall of Agrigentum
	T. Otacilius Crassus	
260 BC	Cn. Cornelius Scipio Asina	Duilius wins sea-fight off Mylae (Milazzo)
	Caius Duilius	
259 BC	L. Cornelius Scipio	War extends to Corsica and Sardinia
	C. Aquillius Florus	
258 BC	A. Atilius Caiatinus	Paterculus wins sea-fight off Sulci, Sardinia
	C. Sulpicius Paterculus	
257 BC	C. Atilius Regulus	Regulus wins sea-fight off Tyndaris
	Cn. Cornelius Blasio	
256 BC	L. Manlius Vulso Longus	Consuls win sea-fight off Ecnomus
	Quintus Caecidius (dies)	
	M. Atilius Regulus *suffectus* (II)	
255 BC	Ser. Fulvius Paetinus Nobilior	Regulus defeated by Xanthippos in Africa
	M. Aemilius Paullus	
254 BC	Cn. Cornelius Scipio Asina (II)	Consuls take Panormus (Palermo)
	A. Atilius Caiatinus	
253 BC	Cn. Servilius Caepio	Roman fleet wrecked off Cape Palinurus
	C. Sempronius Blaesus	
252 BC	C. Aurelius Cotta	Consuls take Lipara and Thermae
	P. Servilius Geminus	
251 BC	L. Caecilius Metellus	Carthaginians reinforce Sicily
	C. Furius Pacilus	
250 BC	C. Atilius Regulus (II)	Consuls commence siege of Libybaeum
	L. Manlius Vulso Longus (II)	
249 BC	P. Claudius Pulcher	Carthaginian naval victory off Drepana
	L. Iunius Pullus	
	A. Atilius Caiatinus (dict.)	
	L. Caecilius Metellus (*mag. equ.*)	
248 BC	C. Aurelius Cotta (II)	Consuls continue to besiege Libybaeum
	P. Servilius Geminus (II)	
247 BC	L. Caecilius Metellus (II)	Hamilcar Barca lands in Sicily
	N. Fabius Buteo	
246 BC	M. Otacilius Crassus (II)	Hamilcar at Heirkte (Monte Castellachio)
	M. Fabius Licinus	

Date	Consuls	Events
245 BC	M. Fabius Buteo	Low-intensity conflict continues in Sicily
	C. Atilius Balbus	
244 BC	A. Manlius Torquatus Atticus	Hamilcar shifts to Eryx (Monte San Giuliano)
	C. Sempronius Blaesus (II)	
243 BC	C. Fundanius Fundulus	Skirmishing persists around Eryx
	C. Sulpicius Galus	
242 BC	C. Lutatius Catulus	New Roman fleet commissioned
	A. Postumius Albinus	
241 BC	A. Manlius Torquatus Atticus (II)	Lutatius wins decisively off Aegates Islands
	Q. Lutatius Cerco	
240 BC	C. Claudius Centho	Hamilcar's veterans revolt (Mercenary War)
	M. Sempronius Tuditanus	
239 BC	C. Mamilius Turrinus	
	Q. Valerius Falto	
238 BC	Ti. Sempronius Gracchus	Rome annexes Sardinia
	P. Valerius Falto	
237 BC	L. Cornelius Lentulus Caudinius	Hamilcar sent to Iberia
	Q. Fulvius Flaccus	
236 BC	P. Cornelius Lentulus Caudinus	Gallic raids on northern Italy
	C. Licinius Varus	
235 BC	T. Manlius Torquatus	
	C. Atilius Balbus (II)	
234 BC	L. Postumius Albinus	
	Sp. Carvilius Maximus	
233 BC	Q. Fabius Maximus Cunctator	
	M. Pomponius Matho	
232 BC	M. Aemilius Lepidus	Bill carried to distribute *ager Gallicus*
	M. Publicius Malleolus	
231 BC	M. Pomponius Matho	Roman embassy to Hamilcar
	C. Papirius Maso	
230 BC	M. Aemilius Bardula	
	M. Iunius Pera	
229 BC	L. Postumius Albinus (II)	Death of Hamilcar
	Cn. Fulvius Centumalus	
228 BC	Sp. Carvilius Maximus (II)	
	Q. Fabius Maximus Cunctator (II)	
227 BC	P. Valerius Flaccus	Caius Flaminius first governor of Sicily
	M. Atilius Regulus	
226 BC	M. Valerius Messalla	Hasdrubal the Splendid signs Iber treaty
	L. Apustius Fullo	
225 BC	L. Aemilius Paullus Papus	Consuls defeat Gauls at Telamon, Etruria
	C. Atilius Regulus	
224 BC	T. Manlius Torquatus (II)	
	Q. Fulvius Flaccus (II)	
223 BC	Caius Flaminius	Flaminius defeats Insubres and Cenomani
	P. Furius Philus	
222 BC	M. Claudius Marcellus	Insubres defeated at Clastidium
	Cn. Cornelius Scipio Calvus	
221 BC	P. Cornelius Scipio Asina	Hasdrubal the Splendid assassinated
	M. Minucius Rufus	
220 BC	L. Venturius Philo	Construction of via Flaminia
	C. Lutatius Catulus	
219 BC	L. Aemilius Paullus	Hannibal Barca takes Saguntum
	M. Livius Salinator	
218 BC	P. Cornelius Scipio	Hannibal marches to Italy (Ticinus, Trebbia)
	Ti. Sempronius Longus	

Date	Consuls	Events
217 BC	Cn. Servilius Geminus Caius Flaminius (II) M. Atilius Regulus *suffectus* (II) Q. Fabius Maximus Cunctator (dict.) M. Minucius Rufus (*mag. equ.*)	Flaminius defeated and killed at Trasimene
216 BC	L. Aemilius Paullus (II) C. Terentius Varro M. Iunius Pera (dict.) Ti. Sempronius Longus (*mag. equ.*)	Hannibal wins decisively at Cannae
215 BC	Q. Fabius Maximus Cunctator (III) Ti. Sempronius Gracchus	Alliance between Carthage and Philip V
214 BC	Q. Fabius Maximus Cunctator (IV) M. Claudius Marcellus (II)	Defection of Syracuse to Carthage
213 BC	Q. Fabius Maximus Minor Ti. Sempronius Gracchus (II)	Marcellus besieges Syracuse
212 BC	Ap. Claudius Pulcher Q. Fulvius Flaccus (III)	Marcellus captures Syracuse
211 BC	P. Sulpicius Galba Maximus Cn. Fulvius Centumalus Maximus	Romans retake Capua
210 BC	M. Valerius Laevinus M. Claudius Marcellus (III)	P. Cornelius Scipio (Africanus) in Iberia
209 BC	Q. Fabius Maximus Cunctator (V) Q. Fulvius Flaccus (IV)	Fabius recaptures Tarentum
208 BC	T. Quinctius Crispinus M. Claudius Marcellus (IV)	Scipio defeats Hasdrubal Barca at Baecula
207 BC	C. Claudius Nero M. Livius Salinator (II)	Hasdrubal defeated and killed at the Metaurus
206 BC	L. Veturius Philo Q. Caecilius Metellus	Scipio wins decisive victory at Ilipa
205 BC	P. Cornelius Scipio Africanus P. Licinius Crassus Dives	Mago Barca invades Italy
204 BC	M. Cornelius Cethegus P. Sempronius Tuditanus	Scipio invades Africa
203 BC	Cn. Servilius Caepio C. Servilius Geminus	Scipio wins victory at Great Plains
202 BC	Ti. Claudius Nero M. Servilius Pulex Geminus	Scipio defeats Hannibal at Zama
201 BC	Cn. Cornelius Lentulus P. Aelius Paetus	Peace formally concluded
200 BC	P. Sulpicius Galba Maximus (II) C. Aurelius Cotta	Start of Second Macedonian War

Ancient authors

Only the most frequently cited ancient authors are listed here. Further details about them, and information about other sources, is most conveniently available in *The Oxford Classical Dictionary* (third edition). In the following notes Penguin denotes Penguin Classics and Loeb denotes Loeb Classical Library. The Loeb editions, which are published by Harvard University Press, display an English translation of a text next to the original language. As Virginia Woolf rightly said, 'the Loeb Library, with its Greek or Latin on one side of the page and its English on the other, came as a gift of freedom ... the existence of the amateur was recognised by the publication of this Library'. For the complete index of Loeb editions you should log on to www.hup.harvard.edu/loeb.

The most important ancient sources for any study of the Second Punic War are, of course, Polybios and Livy (Titus Livius). Sadly, the *Histories* of Polybios has not survived the ravages of time, only five of 40 books survive intact, so his coverage is at times patchy compared with that of Livy. Polybios' style of writing may not compare with that of Livy, but he has the inestimable value of sticking to the facts rather than using large doses of imagination. Moreover, there are times when you feel you could do without the tedious, interminable speeches that Livy inevitably invents for the *dramatis personae* in any major action.

Of course, it is important to remember that for the Greeks and Romans history was a branch of literature intended to entertain as well as inform and inspire. So Livy, despite his obvious shortcomings, has his uses as long as his *History of Rome* is treated with a certain amount of caution. Both of these authors' works are available in Penguin and Loeb. Among other ancient authors, Appian (Appianus), Cassius Dio (Dio Cassius Cocceianus) and Diodoros Siculus are helpful. From the point of view of military affairs, out of the three Appian probably contributes the most, particularly on numbers.

Appian (b. AD 95)

Appian was an Alexandrian Greek who rose to high office in his native city, and appears to have practised law in Rome, where he pleaded cases before the emperors Hadrian (r. AD 117–38) and Antoninus Pius (r. AD 138–61). He composed his *Roman Affairs (Romaika)*, of which the *Hannibalic War* is but a small part, sometime during the reign of Antoninus Pius, at the height of the period that Edward Gibbon aptly labelled 'the golden age of the Antonines'. Appian's target audience was the cultured Greek-speaking privileged elite of the eastern Mediterranean, who had long been not merely affected by Roman rule, but also deeply involved with its workings. Some of its members had already become Roman senators and even consuls, while many more, like Appian himself, had benefited from imperial patronage. But although Rome had established a secure world order, it remained a foreign power, its history generally little understood or appreciated by men who had been brought up on the Greek classics and did not subscribe to quite the same values as their political masters.

Twenty-four books in length, Appian's account of Roman history is essentially a narrative of conquest and struggle, and therefore a narrative of war. His fundamental aim is to paint a clear picture of the relationship of the Romans to the various nations whom they brought under their sway. This leads him to break up his narrative in such a way that each book deals with the interaction of Rome and a particular ethnic group. Nonetheless, he follows a fairly clear chronological scheme, placing the books in the order in which the various peoples first clashed with the Romans. For our purposes the sections dealing with the Punic Wars are intact. Unfortunately, however, these vary considerably in their style, with his battle narratives, in particular, leaving much to desire. His account of Cannae, for example, bears little or no resemblance to those of Polybios or Livy, while his description of Zama reads like an extract from the *Iliad*. There is a Loeb translation of Appian's work.

Cassius Dio (b. AD 164)

Cassius Dio was the author of an 80-book history of Rome from the legendary landing of Aeneas in Italy to the reign of Severus Alexander (AD 222–35). Although he came from Nicaea in Bithynia, Dio belonged to a senatorial family, his father having been proconsul of Cilicia and Dalmatia. Dio's own senatorial career was equally distinguished, praetor in AD 194 and consul *suffectus* probably in AD 205. For ten years from AD 218 he was successively overseer (*curator*) of Pergamum and Smyrna, proconsul of Africa and legate (*legatus*) first of Dalmatia and then of Pannonia Superior, with two legions under his command. In AD 229 he held the ordinary consulship with Severus Alexander as colleague, but retired to his native city almost at once, ostensibly for reasons of ill health, to die at an unknown date. Dio lived through turbulent times: he and his fellow senators quailed before tyrannical emperors and lamented the rise of men they regarded as upstarts, while in Pannonia Superior he grappled with the problem of military indiscipline.

These experiences are vividly evoked in his account of his own epoch and helped shape his view of earlier periods. Like its author, the work is an amalgam of Greek and Roman elements. Titled *Roman Affairs* (*Romaika*), it is written in Attic Greek, with much studied antithetical rhetoric and frequent borrowings from the classical authors, above all the great Athenian historian, Thucydides. The debt to Thucydides is more than merely stylistic: like him, Dio is constantly alert to discrepancies between appearances and reality, truth and allegation. However, in its structure his work revives the Roman tradition of annalistic record of civil and military affairs arranged by consular year. Only the books covering the years 68 BC to AD 46 have come down to us intact, while some idea of the rest can be gained from summaries made in the Byzantine era, notably the epitome made by the early 12th-century monk Zonaras. There is a Loeb translation of Dio's work.

Diodoros Siculus (b. c.80 BC)

A Greek historian who was born at Agyrrhion on Sicily, hence his nickname Siculus, 'the Sicilian', Diodoros eventually left the island to live in Rome. It was here, during the final years of the Roman Republic, that he wrote the *Library* (*Bibliotheke*), a universal history of the Mediterranean world in 40 books from the earliest times to the period of Caesar's conquest of Gaul. Designed to set on record the histories and traditions of various peoples Rome had brought under its rule by the time Diodoros wrote, his *magnum opus* was in three parts – mythical history of peoples, non-Greek and Greek, to the Trojan War; history to Alexander's death (323 BC); history to 54 BC. Of this we have books one to five (Egyptians, Assyrians, Ethiopians, Greeks); books 11 to 20 (Greek history 480 BC to 302 BC); and fragments of the rest.

Diodoros likes to moralize and thus his treatment of history is in truth a series of connected biographies. Although he is somewhat over-imaginative at times and often untrustworthy, his work is extremely useful in that it provides an alternative tradition of events, especially for early Roman history when we are otherwise rather at the mercy of his near-contemporary, Livy. Moreover, his value lies in the fact that he clearly based his work on earlier historians whose text has not survived, notably Philinos' pro-Carthaginian account of the First Punic War, or has survived only in small fragments. There is a Loeb translation of Diodoros' work.

Bibliography

Astin, A. E., 1967, 'Saguntum and the origins of the Second Punic War', *Latomus* 26: 577–96

Bath, T., 1981, *Hannibal's Campaigns*, Cambridge: Patrick Stephens

de Beer, G., 1967, *Hannibal's March*, London: Sidgwick & Jackson

de Beer, G., 1969, *Hannibal*, London: Thames & Hudson

Bell, M. J. V., 1965, 'Tactical reform in the Roman republican army', *Historia* 14: 404–22

Bishop, M. C., and Coulston, J. C. N., 1993, *Roman Military Equipment from the Punic Wars to the Fall of Rome*, London: Batsford

Brunt, P. A., 1971, *Italian Manpower 225 BC–AD 14*, Oxford: Oxford University Press

Cornell, T. J., 1995, *The Beginnings of Rome*, London: Routledge

Cornell, T. J., Rankin, B., and Sabin, P. (eds.), 1996, *The Second Punic War: A Reappraisal*, London: University of London Press (Bulletin of the Institute of Classical Studies 67)

Daly, G., 2002, *Cannae: The Experience of Battle in the Second Punic War*, London: Routledge

Feugère, M., 1993, *Les armes romains de la république à l'antiquité tardive*, Paris: Editions du Centre national de la recherché scientifique

Frederiksen, M. W., 1984, *Campania*, London: British School at Rome

Goldsworthy, A. K., 2000A, *Roman Warfare*, London: Cassell

Goldsworthy, A. K., 2000B, *The Punic Wars*, London: Cassell

Goldsworthy, A. K., 2001, *Cannae*, London: Cassell

Goldsworthy, A. K., 2003, *The Complete Roman Army*, London: Thames & Hudson

Hopkins, K., 1978, *Conquerors and Slaves*, Cambridge: Cambridge University Press

Jones, B. W., 1972, 'Rome's relationship with Carthage: a study in aggression', *The Classical Bulletin* 49: 5–26

Keppie, L. J. F, 1984 (repr. 1998), *The Making of the Roman Army: From Republic to Empire*, London: Routledge

Lazenby, J. F., 1978 (repr. 1998), *Hannibal's War: A Military History of the Second Punic War*, Warminster: Aris & Phillips

Lazenby. J. F., 1996, *The First Punic War: A Military History*, London: University College London Press

Nillson, M. P., 1929, 'The introduction of hoplite tactics at Rome', *Journal for Roman Studies* 19: 1–11

Oakley, S., 1993, 'The Roman conquest of Italy', in J. Rich and G. Shipley (eds.), *War and Society in the Roman World*, London: Routledge, 9–37

Ogilvie, R. M., 1976, *Early Rome and the Etruscans*, Glasgow: Glasgow University Press

Rawlings, L., 1999, 'Condottieri and clansmen: early Italian raiding, warfare and the state', in K. Hopkins (ed.), *Organised Crime in Antiquity*, London: Duckworth, 97–127

Rawson, E., 1971, 'The literary sources for the pre-Marian Roman army', *Papers for the British School at Rome* 39: 13–31

Ridley, R. J., 1975, 'Was Scipio Africanus at Cannae?' *Latomus* 34: 161–65

Sumner, G. V., 1967, 'Roman policy in Spain before the Hannibalic War', *Harvard Studies in Classical Philology* 72: 205–46

Sumner, G.V., 1970, 'The legion and the centuriate organization', *Journal of Roman Studies* 60: 61–78

Wise T., and Healy, M., 1999 (repr. 2002), *Hannibal's War with Rome: The Armies and Campaigns 216 BC*, Oxford: Osprey

Zhmodikov, A., 2000, 'Roman republican heavy infantryman in battle (IV–II centuries BC)'. *Historia* 49: 67–78

Glossary

Acies	line-of-battle
Ager publicus	'public land' – state-owned land acquired by conquest
Agmen	line-of-march
Ala/alae	'wing' – Latin/Italian unit comparable to *legio* (q.v.)
As/asses	small copper coin, worth 1/10th of *denarius* (q.v.)
AUC	*ab urbe condita* (from the foundation of the city), reckoned from 21 April 753 BC
Centuria/centuriae	administrative subunit of *manipulus* (q.v.)
Centurio/centuriones	officer in command of *centuria* (q.v.)
Cohors/cohortes	contingent of infantry from allied community
Decurio/decuriones	officer in command of *turma* (q.v.)
Denarius/denarii	silver coin, worth ten asses, first issued in 211 BC
Imperium	coercive power of higher magistrates
Manipulus/manipuli	'handful' – tactical subunit of *legio* (q.v.)
Legio/legiones	'levy' – principal unit of Roman army
Optio/optiones	second-in-command of *centuria/turma* (q.v.)
Praetorium	consul's tent
Quaestorium	quaestor's tent
Suffectus	'substitute' – consul elected to replace another who died in office
Tribunus/tribuni	'tribal leader' – military tribune
Turma/turmae	tactical subunit of cavalry

Index

References to illustrations are shown in **bold**.

Adherbal **15**
Aegates Islands, battle of (241 BC) 15
Aequi hill-tribe 5
Aetolians 38
Agathokles of Syracuse 9, 11
Agrigentum, siege of (262–261 BC) 54, 55, **56**
Ahenobarbus, Domitius, Altar of **4**, 19, **22**, **34**, **35**, **40**
Akrotatos 9
Albinus, L. Postumius **65**
alae (*socii* military wing) **29**, 29, 49, 75, **79**, 80
Alexander the Great **12**, 58
Alexander the Molossian 9
Allia river 6
allied troops (*socii*) 28–30, 35, 42, 49
Anicius, Marcus 29
Antiochos III 59
Archidamos 9
Archimedes **55**, 56, 63

Britomarus **68**
Brundisium (Brindisi) 10, 28

Campani people 6, 7, 11, 51
Campania 6, 7
camps, marching 52–53
Cannae, battle of (216 BC) 30, 39, 40, 42, 49, 58, 63, 75–77, **76**, 81, 86–87
Capua 7, 63
    siege and battle of (212–211 BC) 51, 54, 86
Carthage 10, **13**, 15, 57, 63, 69, 81
    siege of (149–146 BC) 54
Carthaginian Army 70, **71**, 73, **74**, 75, 76, 77, 80
Carthaginians 11, **13**, 14–15, 58, 61, 63, 66, 81
Cato, M. Porcius (the Censor) 24, 26, 38, 46
Caudine Forks, battle of (321 BC) 7
cavalry, allied 29, 30
cavalry, *equites* 16, **18**, **20**, 24, 26–27, **40**, 51
    see also horsemen
    officers (*decuriones*) 24, **25**, 39
    seconds-in-command (*optiones*) 24, **25**, **37**, 39
    tactical subunits (*turmae*) 24, **25**, 30

Celts **8**
    see also Iberians
Cenomani tribe 29, **71**, 72
census 4, 5, 16
centuriate 36–39
centuries 36, **37**
centurions 36–40, **37**, 42
cinerary urns 9, **14**, **26**, **38**, **47**
citizen-militia 6, 17–18, **18**, 27, 41
clan-armies 4–5
clerk **4**
cohortes (*socii* tactical subunits) **29**, 30
coins **7**, **66**
colonies **8**
comitia centuriata ('assembly in centuries') 5–6, 24, 26–27, 33
command and control (*imperium*) 31–40
    in action 39–40
    legion command 33–36
consuls 31, 32, 33, 36, 39, 40, 62
Cossus, A. Cornelius **68**

dictators 32, **33**, 33
Drepana, battle of (249 BC) **15**, 15
Ducarius 73

elephants, war **57**, **59**, **66**, 69, 70, 72, 77, **79**, **82**, 85
engineering 52–56
equipment
    armour 17, 19, **22**, **35**, **40**, **43**, **46**, **47**, **85**
    cavalry **26**
    Hellenistic **5**
    helmets **11**, **17**, 19, **22**, **28**, **29**, **30**, **38**, **40**, **47**
    hoplite 5, **6**
    shields **4**, 19, **22**, 24, **26**, 48–49
Eryx (Monte San Giuliano) **14**
Etruscan horsemen **26**, **38**, **47**
Etrusci people 6, **8**, **9**, 9, **14**, **16**, 29, 54
extraordinarii (*socii* detached corps) **29**, **30**, 30, 49

Fabii clan-army **4**
Fabius Maximus Cunctator, Q. **33**, 33, **65**
Flaccus, Q. Fulvius 38, **67**
Flamen, Q. Claudius **67**
Flaminius, Caius 32, 36, **64**, **65**, **73**, 73, **74**
Frentani people 29

Gauls 6, 9, **12**, **50**, **51**

Greeks **8**, **12**
guard commander (*tesserarius*) **37**, 39

Hamilcar Barca **14**, 57, 58, 59–60, 61
Hannibal Barca 28, 33, 42, 57, **58**, 58, **59**, 86, 87
    aims of 61–62
    revenge of 59–61
    and Second Punic War 62–63, 64, 66, 68
        Cannae 75, **76**, 76, 86
        Lake Trasimene 72, **73**, 73, **74**, 75
        the Trebbia 70, **71**, 72
        Zama 81, **83**, 84, 85
Hasdrubal, son of Gisgo 64, 80–81, **82**
Hasdrubal Barca 64, 66, 68, 77, **79**, 81
Hasdrubal the Splendid 58, 59–60
Hernici hill-tribe 5
Hieron II of Syracuse 11, 15
honours, *coronae civicae* 38
horsemen **26**, **38**, **46**, **47**, **61**, **63**
    see also cavalry, *equites*

Iapygii people 29
Iber (Ebro), river 60, 61
Iberia 27, 38, 57, 58, 62, 64, 66, 80–81
Iberians (Celtiberi) **12**, 19, **60**, **61**
Ilipa, battle of (206 BC) 80–81, **82**
Illyrian campaign 72
infantry, heavy 19
    hastati 16, **18**, 19, **20**, 22, **23**, 24, **37**, 42, 43, **45**, 46, 48, 85
    principes 16, 17, **18**, 19, **20–21**, 22, **23**, 24, **37**, 42, **45**, 48
    triarii 16, **18**, 19, **21**, 22, **23**, 24, **37**, 42, 48, 53
infantry, light (*velites*) 16, **18**, 24, 42, **44**, 50–51, 70, 72, 80, 85
Italian Peninsula, 3rd century BC **8**
Italians 28–29
Italy 6–7, 9–10, 53–54, 62–63, 64, 66, 68

Kleonymos 9

Latin War (341–338 BC) 7
Latini people 6, **8**, 28, 29
Latium 6, 7
legionaries **22**, **35**, **36**, **46**, 46
legions (*legiones*) 16, **18**, 24, **44**, 86
    in battle 42–43, 46–49
    Cannenses (penal legions) **70**, **83**
    command 33–36
    consular (I to IIII) 32

deployment, three-line (*triplex acies*)
  20, **21**, 42, 80
  close-order **23**
legiones I and III 32, 34, **63**, **64**, **65**, **67**,
  69, **79**
legiones II and IIII 32, 34, **63**, **64**, **65**,
  67, **69**
legiones V and VI **63**, **64**, **70**, **82**, **83**
legiones XVIIII and XX **67**, **69**
Livian description 16–17
manipular 7, 16, **44–45**
Polybian description 17–18
Licinus, L. Porcius **67**, **77**, **79**
Ligustinus, Spurius 37–39
Lilybaeum **15**
Lucani people 6–7, **8**, 29
Lusitani people **12**

Macedonian War, Second (200–197 BC)
  37–38
Macedonians 19, 26, **46**
magistrates 31, 32, 35–36
magistrates' lictors **31**, 32
Mago Barca 64, 68, 70, 72, 76, 81, **82**
Maharbal 86
Mamertini 11, 14
maniples (*manipuli* – tactical subunits)
  20–21, **22**, 22, **23**, 24, 30, 36, 42,
  49, 53, 80
manipular system 7, 16, **44–45**
Marcellus, M. Claudius 55, **68**, 68–69
Mars **34**
Marsi people 29
Marucini people 29
Masinissa **83**, 85
Mediterranean basin, 3rd century BC
  12–13
Messana (Messina), seizure of *polis* of 11, 14
Messapii people 29
Metaurus, river, battle of (207 BC) 66, 68,
  77, **79**
Metellus, Q. Caecilius **69**
Miccalus, Ti. Flavius 36
milestones 54
Minucius Rufus, M. 33

Naples (Neapolis) 7
navies 15
Nero, C. Claudius 66, **67**, 68, **77**, **79**
New Carthage, siege of (209 BC) 54
Numantia, siege of (134–133 BC) 19, 54
Numidians **63**, 70, **71**, 72, 76, 85

oath, military 18
officers, junior 39
Oscan-speaking peoples 6–7, **8**

Paullus, L. Aemilius 40, **46**, **65**, 72, 76,
  77, **78**
phalanx, Greek-style 5, 7, 16, 49
Philip V of Macedon 62, 63
Philo, L. Veturius **69**
Porcius, Marcus 24, 26, 38, 46
praefecti sociorum (*socii* officer) **29**, 29, 39
praetors (magistrates) 32, 35–36
Pulcher, P. Claudius **15**
Punic War, First 11, 14–15, 19
Punic War, Second 27, 57, 59–64, 66,
  68–70, 72–73, 75–77, 80–81, 84–85
  Cannae 30, 39, 40, 42, 49, 58, 63,
    75–77, **76**, 81, 86–87
  Hannibal's aims 61–62
  Hannibal's revenge 59–61
  Ilipa 80–81, **82**
  Lake Trasimene 36, 63, 72–73, **73**,
    74, 75
  the long struggle 62–64, 66, 68–69
  the Metaurus 66, 68, 77, **79**
  the Trebbia 24, 29, 63, 70, **71**, 72
  Zama 69, 81, **83**, **84**, 84–85, 86
punishment 36
Pyrrhic War (280–275 BC) 17
Pyrrhos of Epeiros 9, **13**, 52, **57**

quaestors 36

Regulus, M. Atilius 75–76, **78**
Rhegion (Reggio di Calabria) 11
roads 32, **52**, 53–54
Roman Army
  in battle 41–43, 46–51
    cavalry 51
    legion 42–43, 46–49
    light troops 50–51
    manipular tactics **44–45**
    tactical doctrine and practice 42
  military organization 16–19, 22, 24,
    26–27, **63**, **64**, **65**, **67**, **69**, **70**
  socii 28–30, 35, 42, 49
Rome 5, 6, 86

Sabini hill-tribe 5, 6, 29
Saguntum (Sagunto) 60–61
Salinator, M. Livius 66, **67**, 68, **69**, 77, **79**
Samnite Wars, First (343–341 BC) and
  Second (327–304 BC) 7
Samnite War, Third (298–290 BC) 9, 19
Samnites 7, **8**, 9, **10**, 16, **18**, 29, 87
Samnium (Abruzzi) 7, 9
Sarsinati people 29
Schlieffen, Count Alfred von 75
Scipio, P. Cornelius 40, **63**, 64, 66
Scipio Aemilianus, P. Cornelius 54, 55, 72

Scipio (Africanus), P. Cornelius 66, 69, **70**,
  71, 80, **81**, 81, **82**, **83**, 85
Scipio Calvus, Cn. Cornelius 64, 64, 66
Sempronius Longus, Ti. **63**, 70, **71**, 72
Senate 14, 17, 28, 29, 31–32, 62
Senonian Gauls 6, 9
Sentinum, battle of (295 BC) 9
Serranus, C. Atilius **63**, **65**
Servilius Geminus, Cn. **64**, **65**, 76, 77, **78**
Sicily 10, 15, 27, 30, 36, 58, 63, **69**
siegecraft 54–56
socii military organization 28–30, 35, 42, 49
standard-bearer (*signifer*) **37**, 39
Syracuse, siege, assault and retaking of
  (213–212 BC) 54, **55**, 55–56, 63–64
Syrian War (192–189 BC) 38

Taras (Taranto), sack of (272 BC) 9, 10, 14
Tarentum 63
Telamon, battle of (225 BC) 48
Trapani **14**, **15**
Trasimene, Lake, battle of (217 BC) 36,
  63, 72–73, **73**, **74**, 75
treaties 28
Trebbia, battle of the (218 BC) 24, 29, 63,
  70, **71**, 72
tribuni militum **18**, 24, 33–35, **34**, 39,
  40, **44**
trumpeter (*cornicen*) **37**, 39
Tubulus, C. Hostilius 67
Tullius, Servius **4**, 5
Turrinus, Q. Mamilius **69**

Umbri people 9, 29

Vachères warrior **43**
Varro, C. Terentius **65**, **67**, **69**, 75, 76,
  77, **78**
Veii 54
Veneti people 29
Vestini people 29
via Appia **52**
Volsci hill-tribe 5
Vulso, L. Manlius **63**, **65**

warriors **6**, **10**, **14**, **18**, **43**, **50**, **51**, **60**
weapons
  cavalry 26
  dagger (*pugio*) 19
  Gallic **48**
  javelins 24
  spears **16**, 17, 19, 42–43
  swords 19, 24, 26, **36**, 41, 46–48, **48**, **60**

Zama, battle of (202 BC) 69, 81, **83**, **84**,
  84–85, 86